About the Microsoft Network Series

THE MICROSOFT ALUMNI NETWORK is a worldwide community of former employees who share a common experience of having worked at Microsoft. Founded in 1995, the Alumni Network is a member organization representing more than fifty thousand alumni in fifty-one countries. The Alumni Network publishing partnership with HarperCollins Leadership represents the broad range of talent that makes up the Microsoft alumni community: entrepreneurs, tech innovators, business professionals, nonprofit leaders, volunteers, and lifelong learners, while shining a light on the meaningful impact that Microsoft's alumni have around the globe.

LISTING OF SERIES BOOKS:

THE

SWIPE-RIGHT

CUSTOMER
EXPERIENCE

HOW TO ATTRACT, ENGAGE, AND KEEP CUSTOMERS IN THE DIGITAL-FIRST WORLD

SANNA ESKELINEN & BELINDA GERDT

HarperCollins
Leadership

An Imprint of HarperCollins

Published by HarperCollins Leadership, an imprint of HarperCollins Focus LLC.

Any internet addresses, phone numbers, or company or product information printed in this book are offered as a resource and are not intended in any way to be or to imply an endorsement by HarperCollins Leadership, nor does Harper-Collins Leadership vouch for the existence, content, or services of these sites, phone numbers, companies, or products beyond the life of this book.

ISBN 978-1-4002-3231-4 (eBook)
ISBN 978-1-4002-3230-7 (TP)

Library of Congress Control Number: 2022943564

Printed in the United States of America
22 23 24 25 26 LSC 10 9 8 7 6 5 4 3 2 1

To all organizations that are passionate about creating memorable customer experiences.

And to the next generation of customers— like our children Aino, Anni, and Christofer.

You are our constant source of inspiration.

CONTENTS

INTRODUCTION

The global Covid-19 pandemic forced everybody to rethink how they operate and the role that digital plays in business and in our lives. While digital may have been top of mind for many businesses, the pandemic made it essential, not just as a way to interact and sell products and services, but as a way to meet the critical needs of your business.

Another big impact from the pandemic is that, more than ever before, people are looking for experiences, not products. And not just any experiences, but real experiences that turn transactions into engagement and materialism into experimentalism. The pandemic has changed our view of the world, shifted us away from consumerism and made us appreciate again the basic human needs of finding balance and focus. In this new era, the customer experience is not just a digital experience, but a perfect combination of real life and digital interaction. It could be a meditative museum experience combining art with augmented reality or an entertaining shopping experience at a mall with omni-channel support in a virtual fitting room.

But while the world has been turned upside down and all things digital have accelerated across all sectors, many fundamental principles of the digital customer experience that were in place before the pandemic remain the same. Technology continues to change our behaviors as consumers and citizens. It impacts the way we communicate, search for information and consume products and services. Customers want quick and easy ways to interact and engage with businesses. An increasing number of activities and customer journey steps can now be taken online as processes are becoming more automated and data now enables more personalized and individualized service.

New technology has emerged to remove the more tedious parts of the customer experience. Only a decade ago we were accustomed to waiting and repeating our details several times during the sales process. Now we expect to be served immediately and we expect the customer experience to be seamless. Engaging with businesses and organizations is expected to become faster and easier. Only a few people have the patience to wait for more than a couple of days for goods they have ordered online; it should be possible to get a diagnosis from a medical provider over a video call; and paying a bill should preferably be handled automatically. Queuing in shops will become history soon.

In the 1990s, the internet made it possible to develop digital services. A decade later mobile technology dramatically changed the communication between consumers and businesses. The era of artificial intelligence (AI) is making an impact that will surpass these previous two eras.

Digitalization represents an unprecedented opportunity to businesses and organizations, but it also poses a major challenge. Modern technologies are relatively invisible, and identifying competitors' solutions is difficult. In the past, copying a webpage or a mobile application was fast and cheap. Projects implemented with AI are more challenging to replicate, so when successful they can provide a significant competitive advantage. And success with the digital customer experience is never only about the technology! Businesses need to (re)design their systems and processes around the customer, unify data and (most likely) change their organizational culture and employee mindset. Externally, all these complex multi-year changes will result in more efficient service, smoother interaction, and tailored engagement.

The first three chapters in *The Swipe-Right Customer Experience* get into more detail on how digitalization, emerging technology tools, and leadership requirements change the customer experience game. We have then gathered case studies from leading international businesses and organizations that already leverage customer-centric, innovative solutions and focus on developing the customer experience in the digital era. We touch upon five sectors: retail, retail banking, hospitality and travel, healthcare, and education. The pandemic has accelerated the change much faster than we ever imagined and we hope that this book provides you with new ideas, insights, and strategies for your own journey!

1

DIGITALIZATION AND
CUSTOMER EXPERIENCE

Digitalization has been impacting the business world for decades. For example, the music and entertainment industries were transformed when music, TV shows, and movies moved to digital format and customers migrated from CDs and TV channels to content and streaming platforms. The retail industry was turned upside down when long-standing brick-and-mortar retailers went bust one after the other as consumers moved their shopping online. Video rental shops and travel agencies have vanished almost entirely, and even the world's most traditional universities now offer many courses online.

The first wave of digitalization started many years before the pandemic. It has driven the biggest changes for customer experience and, in turn, changes in businesses. We have traveled a long way from internet to mobile, in about ten years. Digitalization began when web browsers were developed in the mid-1990s and information became widely available. Netscape's and Internet Explorer's battle for market share made browsing popular. In the first phase of digitalization, businesses built websites.

The second phase of digitalization brought an endless number of applications to mobile phones. In the 2000s, smartphones found their way into people's pockets with Apple's lead. Google permanently changed marketing with its search engine, and the importance of digital marketing efforts increased at a fast pace. In 2020, corporate digital ad spending in the US exceeded the traditional channels for the first time. Facebook's, Google's and Amazon's share of this pie was two-thirds![1] Even if mobile changed the way we communicate, search for information and approach customers, it did not transform entire industries. The next phase, which is already at hand, is characterized by more advanced technologies such as artificial intelligence and robotics.

This third phase will change business much more. We are talking about the fourth industrial revolution where digitalization transforms product offerings, core processes, corporate culture, and staff skill profiles, rather than being a stand-alone project or separate technology initiative. When looking at the statements from the World Economic Forum in Davos, for example, most executives said finding new talent and training the existing staff to meet the increasing demands of technology were at the top of their agendas.

Covid-19 smashed all the previous trajectories of speed, scale, and reach of this third wave of digital transformation and the importance of the digital customer experience. According to Adobe's 2021 Digital Trends Report, almost all senior executives (92 percent) agreed that the pandemic increased the priority of digital transformation as well as the importance of speed and agility.[2] We leapfrogged years, if not decades, in customer behavior, mindset and the role of digital in our lives and in business.

From the early days, one of the key characteristics of digitalization has been the large impact a few key players can make on the entire market. The competitive advantage that technology can provide has been so large for so long that it has not been easy to catch up with the leaders: market shares have concentrated to IT giants that have often seen exponential growth and have become platforms for the smaller players.

The next couple of years will show how AI and robotics will change businesses and broader society. Amazon, Microsoft, Google and IBM are leading the pack in the development of modern technologies such as AI. The battle of ecosystems and platforms will accelerate and intensify when businesses that digitalized early will expand into new sectors with the help of their strong processes and loyal customer base.

KEY AREAS OF DEVELOPING THE CUSTOMER EXPERIENCE

While technology evolves rapidly, it is good to remember that the key areas for customer experience development haven't changed (see figure 1). Their importance has only increased. When developing customer experience, businesses should examine all the areas that define their success: the corporate culture, skills, processes and workflow, brand and measurement. The focus in developing these areas has just become technology-assisted due to the increasing role and capabilities of technology.

The key areas for customer experience development				
Culture	**Skills**	**Processes & workflow**	**Brand**	**Measuring**
• Values	• Recruiting	• Utilizing technology	• Value statement	• Ambition
• Empowerment	• Training	• Integration	• Trust	• Continuity
• Decision making	• Leadership	• Transparency	• Uniqueness	• Net Promoter
• Continuous learning	• Resources	• Streamlining	• Recognizability	Score
		• Managing networks	• Relevance	
Technology				

FIGURE 1

The key areas driving customer experience development

Culture

Building a customer-centric business starts with corporate culture and putting the customer at the center of it. The culture sets the company values, guides operation models, and impacts everyday decision making at different levels of the organization. Culture strongly guides actions as it empowers decision making that is directly visible to the customer.

It is also important to emphasize continuous development and learning, especially now when technology is increasing in intensity and the pace of change is accelerating. The culture also needs to take different customer needs into account. Diversity and inclusion should play a prominent role.

Skills

Developing a customer experience requires talent and skill. As sectors transform, customers' purchasing behavior and expectations change and competitors are developing more advanced strategies and operational models. Every business will need not only the ability to understand and manage the change, but also innovation to leverage resources that offer better, more customer-centric products and services to customers.

It is not always easy to find skilled workers, or there isn't a budget for hiring them. Not everything must be done in-house, but there needs to be a strong network of expertise that will help take the organization forward. The importance of the network and platform economy is increased where there is a scarcity of skilled workers. Ensuring skills with training, right recruitments, and competent leadership will be critical as the pace of change accelerates. In addition to skills, there also needs to be a willingness to change.

Processes

Internal processes and operation models have a significant role in developing the customer experience. Businesses are expected to be more efficient, error-free and integrated. The pandemic also demonstrated the value of speed and agility. The fragility of complex supply chains and processes caused businesses to reevaluate how to ensure production and distribution in the event of a crisis.

Developing customer experience includes different communication channels and their seamless integration, continuous availability of service, rapid response times, effective leverage of customer data and proactive pre- and post-service. Data is power and there is constantly more of it available. The organizations that manage to use it best and personalize experiences and responses to changes in consumer behavior will gain competitive advantages.

Brand

As digitalization accelerates, the importance of the corporate brand is emphasized. As customers move to big platforms and portals, they have unlimited options at their fingertips. Comparing prices is easier and algorithms generate more recommendations by filtering information. Building a strong corporate brand image is paramount, and building a direct distribution channel without one is almost impossible.

The brand communicates the company values in a world where the importance of integrity, brand identity and personality are emphasized. Customers want to interact with businesses who they can identify with and that are purpose-driven. Being environmentally friendly, socially conscious, ethical and personal is more important than ever.

Measurement

Creating a customer experience is not effective if you cannot measure it. You will need clear KPIs to indicate the progress you are making and the level of success. There may be plenty of data available, but it is pointless if it is not analyzed and used. One should not get blindsided by different kinds of performance indicators though. It will come as a surprise to many that when change is rapid, the old indicators may still be flashing green while the customer is already unhappy with the old-fashioned products, operating models and services. (For more about measurement see chapter 3.)

ECOSYSTEMS AND PLATFORMS
DEFINING YOUR FUTURE

Very few companies can make it alone in today's rapidly changing world. Building partnerships, networks, communities and ecosystems helps companies to source talent, tap into special expertise, leverage technology investments, innovate business models and build customer experiences beyond organizational boundaries. Leveraging platforms can significantly help companies to shorten the lead time to value creation and concentrate on building their unique offering and business rather than platform capabilities.

The single largest factor that slows the ability of a business to respond to challenges brought about by digitalization is technical expertise. Automation, AI and its applications require expertise that is difficult to find. It is also expensive. Most top experts work for the leading tech giants or their own start-ups. Therefore, the most sensible way to leverage the newest technologies is to partner with innovators, build ecosystems and buy readily available solutions. As a result of the pandemic, many companies have adopted new policies related to remote working and hiring talent outside their usual office locations. Flexible working conditions and opening positions for applications worldwide help companies to reach the right talent, but competition for digital talent remains high. To attract top talent, you have to offer not only competitive benefits, but also an interesting and purposeful vision that motivates the talent to build a business of the future.

When evaluating expertise and its sufficiency, one should also keep in mind diversity in the development teams and make sure that, in addition to technological expertise, there is substance expertise: combining the two will generate the best results. For example, in healthcare a team consisting of doctors and tech experts may be able to come up with results that neither team could on their own. Diversity ensures that the development work avoids the worst pitfalls and the products and services meet the needs of a broad customer base.

Answering the customers' needs requires the expertise to be married to innovative ideas that add value. Automating payments brought Uber a significant competitive advantage. Its technical implementation was not too difficult. Travel giants Booking.com and Airbnb were developed in the same fashion. At the end of the day, the best innovations start from the best ideas to develop better products and experiences for the customer.

The digital revolution at hand differs from the previous waves of internet and mobile due to its complexity. However, adopting different kinds of technologies, such as AI, is inevitable going forward: it will change sectors and strengthen the platform economy.

Platform Economy Will Change How Businesses Operate

The role of platforms will grow and they will have an increasingly large influence. The platform economy changes competition significantly as indirect competition will increase in almost every sector. Well-known tech firms that are platform influencers include Alibaba, Amazon, Apple, eBay, Facebook, and Netflix. Developers can use the platform these firms provide to develop new businesses. Completely new services and service lines will be created at the back of ecosystems and platforms.

> Platform economy is economic and social activity where technological infrastructure and services (by third parties) built on top of it play a central role. This development environment enabled by technology and offered to different parties can be called a platform, and the economic activity taking place on it can be called platform economy.

It is much easier for an aspiring internet retailer to start her business by offering her products on Amazon than to develop her own distribution channel. Competing with the experience that the top firms have is challenging and in addition consumers already spend much of their time with services offered by these giants. Facebook's popularity and whether its position will become shaky has been discussed for a long time, but with 2.5 billion users it is still the world's largest and most popular social media service.

In China, the WeChat service has surpassed a billion users, and almost all payments in China are processed through Alipay and WeChat Pay. While there are still taxis in Europe that only accept cash payments, in China a mobile app is displacing credit cards. Gaming houses develop new games using Microsoft and AWS cloud technologies and ecosystems. It is easier for restaurants to deliver orders to customers with Uber than to build their own logistical chains.

There is hope that the platform economy will provide a solution to the sudden increase in unemployment caused by the pandemic, especially in the service, hospitality and travel sectors.[3] Different kinds of portals offering housekeeping, childcare and other services have provided some relief to the sudden surge in unemployment. Trust in tech brands is higher than ever before. More than half of the world's most valuable brands are tech firms whereas ten years ago the number stood at two or three. The rise in valuation is largely due to increased trust by consumers.[4] Technology has proved that it is reliable and consumers believe that tech firms are able to leverage information and foresee and fix errors.

Squeezed by Portals

From allowing travelers to book their own flights to helping consumers compare utility providers, portals such as Skyscanner and Booking.com have rewritten rulebooks for several industries. They have entered markets where traditional players and established brands have been too slow to provide the digital experiences customers were looking for. The power of the platforms is based on connecting the consumer and the service provider and maintaining this relationship. A strong ecosystem as well as insights-based, continuously adapting marketing and distribution channels are key to their success. These portals can provide consumers with two things that hotels, restaurants, utility providers and many others have not been able to offer alone: alternatives and bargaining power.

The impact of the portals is particularly large in sectors that sell functional products with low emotional attachment.

For example, because consumers seldom have a strong emotional attachment to insurance or energy, the provider is not particularly important to them. It is more important that the service meets the need and the price is right.

Brands that meet the consumers' values and enforce their individuality will find it easier to maintain their position. It will not be easy though. Fewer and fewer consumers on Amazon, for example, search for products from a specific brand. And on the portals, the order of the search results has been programmed by the platform or the portal developer: they do not appear in the order of best match or greatest benefit for the customer. For example, in 2019, Amazon changed its algorithms so as to boost its own products.[5] With virtual assistants becoming more common, we see their recommendations increasingly influence our purchase decisions as well. When customers buy goods directly using voice commands, the search in its current form is eliminated from the purchase process.

Going forward, things will become even more interesting as, for example, home appliances will be able to make orders with the help of their sensors: When your laundry machine orders more detergent, who decides the brand? Initially it might be you, but what happens when that brand is out of stock and the machine has been programmed to order a similar product? Or what if a cheaper product is available?

According to some forecasts, marketing targeted at machines will surpass marketing aimed at people in the coming years. The best way for businesses to ensure future success and to be in the game long term is to partner with the top players in the field. Continuous learning and open-minded testing of new opportunities will help shake customary operational models and develop the customer experience to a level required by the digital revolution.

COMPETITORS: YOUR BEST PARTNERS

Digitalization has shown its strength in many sectors. It is no longer a surprise to any business to see new competitors from outside the sector enter the market. Businesses that have long been operating in the same fashion have not always been able to sufficiently challenge their operating models and remove the deficiencies in the customer experience. You no longer need to return rented videos to the video store, pay with cash or card for rides, or queue at the grocery store when you are tired after a long day at work. None of these improvements in the customer experience were born out of innovations by the incumbents. They required a new, nimble, customer-oriented player.

Digitalization changes the elements that impact competition. Some digital solutions and technologies are difficult or almost impossible to replace with other products. That is why many online stores that compete with Amazon on digital content buy server capacity from this key competitor of theirs.

Competition has also become more diverse. Competitors can simultaneously be each other's customers and part of the same ecosystem, advancing the demand for the entire sector, product or solution. For example, many tech firms are each other's largest customers—while simultaneously being competitors. Growing the overall demand brings all players the largest benefits.

A good example of growth in overall demand are cloud services, which became widely available about a decade ago. Many companies had built their own server solutions that competed with cloud services. The largest cloud players created the prerequisites for growth together by improving information security and availability of the service among other things. As demand grew, the price also continuously decreased.

Different kinds of collaboration opportunities, the platform economy, and complex digital earning models make business operations more diverse: the traditional competitor and customer roles will slowly disappear. Winners will be businesses that can build broad networks and cooperate with the most influential market players.

The Pace of Change Is Accelerating

The pace of change is faster than ever before. The competitive positions can change in months when previously entering a market and gaining a leading position took years, even decades. Digitalization makes it possible to gain a large customer base in a relatively short time. The process also works the other way around. Therefore, questionable actions and the subsequent loss of reputation can destroy even a profitable business in a short time. Social media plays a significant role in this.

Previously, new entrants came in mainly with lower prices in order to attract customers. Now new entrants still bring pricing pressure, but often first and foremost a better customer experience, which the customer perceives as improved quality. Consumers are looking for alternatives and these new entrants almost always leverage the opportunities brought about by digitalization and new technology, which the large, slow mammoths have not been capable of tapping into. By focusing on the customer and removing all unnecessary, non-value-adding parts, they can maximize the price-to-quality ratio.

What makes this situation challenging for businesses is that when digital services are taking their first steps, it is difficult to estimate their impact. Few grocery stores can determine how large of an impact Amazon Go or Alibaba's Hema will have on the sector in a couple of years when cashier-less stores spread across the US and China. The best way to protect oneself from rapid changes in the market is to build a broad network and cooperation agreements that make it possible to benefit from the changes. Frustratingly often, businesses see change as a threat instead of an opportunity when there could be a path to new markets and significant growth in the wake of the digital giants and with the digitally native customers.

New Competitive Forces

Michael Porter's famous five forces model is familiar to most businesses. In the model, industry rivalry is analyzed from the viewpoint of the bargaining power of buyers, the bargaining power of suppliers, the threat of new entrants and the threat of substitutes. The factors of the model get a new shape in the digital-first world.

Previously a company's competitive strategy began with the idea that it was possible to choose between cost leadership and differentiation based on high quality and better customer service. Unfortunately, these times are over. Now every business must do both (see figure 2). Every sector already has trailblazers that have managed to carry this out. Technology increases the ability to streamline processes and leaves time and money to invest in the customer.

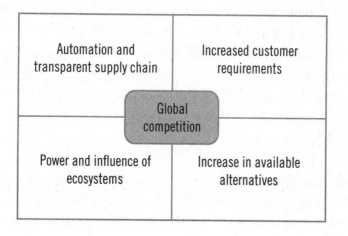

FIGURE 2

Digitalization changes the competitive environment for businesses.

Let's take a look at how these forces are creating a transition.

From new players to the power of the ecosystems. New players enter markets all the time. Often it happens through partnerships or acquisitions. As leading digital platforms and portals actively participate in (and even control) customer decision making, the influence of ecosystem power increases. The platforms and portals control the information customers have at their disposal; they also choose the alternatives shown to customers based on algorithms. It is now more difficult for businesses to present their products directly to customers without taking the influence and power of digital platforms and ecosystems into account.

From customers' bargaining power to increased customer requirements. Previously it was possible for businesses to differentiate themselves by pricing *or* by excellent service. They could offer either more affordable products or quality service that stood out. Now, it is not enough to do one of the two. Customers want competitive prices, new products, and excellent service. As the number of available alternatives has grown, so has the customer's power, making them less loyal to brands and products. In many situations, the customers are in control of the relationship.

From industry rivalry to global rivalry. A couple of decades ago, competition was presumed to be tied to a geographical location or a certain industry. This is no longer the case. Customers can now acquire products and services from anywhere in the world. You can even graduate from an international university online. This alone does not impact global competition; the largest influence comes from the examples the customer sees. A domestic online shop needs to be able to deliver the same customer experience as its global peers. For restaurants and hotels, the customer experiences and purchase experiences have long been rated based on an international scale.

Competitors also often come from other sectors: banking services are offered by furniture retailers and Starbucks, transportation services (like Uber) have no cars, and accommodation services (like Airbnb) have no hotels of their own! Firms that have a broad customer base and technological capabilities are diligently expanding into new sectors.

From supplier bargaining power to transparency of the supply chain. Technology automates the supply chain, improves inventory management and order processes, and offers more data to analyze prices, differences in quality, and other product-specific aspects. Supplier relationships are not only becoming automated, but fully transparent. When inventory management is connected with an order process that automatically activates as inventory falls below a preset level, the supplier-customer relationship requires transparency.

From substitute products to infinite alternatives. Customers have more alternatives available than ever before. Consumer-to-consumer business and the barter economy, which have been enabled by digital channels, provide more alternatives to products offered by global corporations. You no longer have to buy products. You can borrow them, buy them second-hand, or rent them. Customers are moving from products to services. People want to buy almost everything with a monthly subscription service!

CUSTOMERS WANT A RELATIONSHIP

According to Salesforce's "State of the Connected Customer Report 2020," 84 percent of customers said the experience a company provides is as important as its products and services.[6] Think about this: When you order an Uber, do you do it because its cars (Toyota Priuses!) are much better than those from a local taxi-service provider, or because Uber drivers provide exceptional travel experiences? Or is it because ordering the ride, getting real-time information on its arrival, the ease of payment and the overall experience is so smooth?

Digitalization provides an unprecedented opportunity for businesses and organizations to develop the customer experience. Unfortunately, sometimes new technologies create overexcitement and experiences that customers neither want nor need. Almost everything is possible, but do they create real added value for the customer? When a toaster includes an option to print patterns on the bread and send messages to a mobile app during the thirty seconds of toasting, is this a long-anticipated, value-adding service to the customer— especially when it is still possible to burn your toast due to an incorrectly set timer?

Also, technology stapled on a bad product will not salvage a weak customer experience. Technology in and of itself is not actually important: what counts is the end result you seek, with the help of technology. Even the best technology will not provide a way forward if it is poorly adopted.

A good start is to focus on providing a value-adding service and experience that is supported with technology. Beyond a successful transaction and a beautiful moment in time, the customer expects *partnership*. When there are infinite alternatives, the customer chooses the ones that satisfy their deepest expectations, values and emotions. The customer journey has become the life journey.[7] It is not enough to analyze the purchasing journey. Instead of transactional optimization, the customer expects emotional optimization. Behind the purchase experience are our personal dreams, fears and frustrations. We do not only want to "buy" products or services, but we also want businesses to save us time and money, facilitate our aspirations and create memorable life experiences.

Customer expectations are pretty clear. What is striking, though, is the huge gap between the experience companies believe they deliver and how customers perceive and value them. According to Bain & Company, 80 percent of companies believe they deliver superior experiences to customers, but only 8 percent of customers agree.[8] It is important to break the experience down into its core elements and ensure all these building blocks are being developed. Experience is much more than the moment we interact with companies. At best it is a lifelong relationship that lasts, even when the world is changing around us.

THE BUILDING BLOCKS OF CUSTOMER EXPERIENCE

The four core elements of customer experience are a relevant offering, responsiveness, ease of use, and trust and continuity.

Relevant Personalized Offering

A digital customer strategy starts with a relevant offering. We have seen many industries change. Digitalization has already changed entertainment, taxis, retail and hospitality. The next phase will leave no sector quite the same. Developing the customer experience is pointless if none of the products or services are relevant to the customer. Not even the best service will make customers return from Netflix to Blu-ray videos or from mobile banking to checks.

Relevancy also means that products and services are personalized, even individualized. The customer expects increasingly more personal recommendations and service based on things such as previous purchases, health concerns or learning history. It is no longer enough that the experience feels personal. It must *be* personal. Your name printed on the corner of a direct marketing letter is seen as awkward. Digital customer experiences are built on a promise of personalization, yet are challenged by multiple sources of customer data, legacy IT systems and the inability to use data effectively. With larger data sets, AI and machine learning, we have an opportunity to transform segmentation by moving from personalization to real-time individualization, from tailoring messages to groups to creating one-to-one communication and engagement.

Product personalization will also continue to grow strongly. Customers already order customized clothes, shoes and bags from different brands. In addition, Sounds Like You by Pandora is an experiential music service where you can customize a song just for you.

Responsiveness

Nowadays the only time people do not have access to online services is when the battery of their mobile device is out. We expect service to be available 24/7. Previously it was enough that a product purchased online would reach the customer in a week. Now the customer expects to receive it in an hour. A message left at Customer Service used to take several days to get through, now the customer expects to receive an answer on a question she has posted on social media immediately. The three bouncing balls in a chat window have become the standard expectation. We want to feel that somebody is there, already typing an answer to us.

Five years ago, KLM Royal Dutch Airlines was one of the first businesses to promise a response on a customer service query in an hour. Now KLM offers a virtual assistant that helps you pack based in part on destination weather information. They also have an augmented reality service that offers "travel" to the destination beforehand while you are still at the airport.

Marketing and customer communication are becoming increasingly automated. Automating marketing has progressed far already and there are many technologies available to develop it. Automation goes hand in hand with personalization. Offering real-time information and automated reactions to customer behavior will improve the customer experience and benefit the business.

Customer communication becomes automated as part of developing marketing and customer service. Often communication to customers means announcements, such as flight information, an upcoming change of tires or a delay in service delivery. Communication changes significantly with new interfaces, such as voice-controlled APIs. This gives the business new opportunities for a dialogue with customers and a chance to improve the customer experience.

Ease of Use

Nowadays everything has to be convenient and effortless: payments, transactions, customer service. We no longer want to wait, and standing in line will disappear altogether. Purchasing will be split into two categories. We will want to automate all purchases where there is a low emotional bond. All the rest should provide experiences. We would like toilet paper to just appear in the cupboard, but when we go shopping on a weekend, we are ready to spend hours in a store.[9] Increasingly, more specialized boutiques have coffee shops and additional rewards to keep us there.

New kinds of interfaces from voice control to virtual reality (VR) will require new kinds of thinking around customer friendliness. Technology should be easy to use and the purchase experience intuitive. Easy usability will become the most important factor of customer loyalty. Research has clearly shown the connection between ease of use and high customer loyalty. When transactions become cumbersome, loyalty decreases.

Trust and Continuity

As with all human relationships, trust is the key factor influencing customer commitment to a company, service or brand. We want our transactions to meet certain expectations. We appreciate guaranteed availability of service, standardized quality, predictability and trustworthiness. (This is evidenced by the success of franchises, even if products and services of better quality are available elsewhere for a lower price!) We want to know what we can expect because it increases our sense of security. Of course, we want to be surprised by excellent service, but after each experience our expectations go up and the next time should be as surprising!

Most people trust technology, but the trust is eroded quickly if systems don't provide almost 100 percent reliability. According to various surveys, the expected "sufficient level" of reliability of digital services such as a booking systems, online shops and mobile apps is incredibly high.

It is believed that in the future, technology will diagnose our illnesses more accurately, robots will give better investment recommendations and virtual assistants will provide better service. Research has shown that customers trust technology more than humans as long as the technology functions seamlessly. When navigation systems became common in cars, most people still used paper maps and relied on their traveling companion to navigate, just to be on the safe side. As technology evolved and reliability increased, the GPS became a standard feature in cars; nowadays most drivers trust the technology more than they trust human navigators. The same path lies ahead with self-driving cars. Once a sufficient development level has been achieved, customers will prefer a service experience provided by a machine.

Developing the customer experience of the digital age is challenging without proper IT infrastructure. Nowadays it is difficult to name even a single process that generates a customer experience where technology does not play a role. Even sectors like hospitality that pride themselves on personal customer service rely on background systems as they build a smooth customer experience and continuity of service. To ensure a personalized experience, the customers must be identified and their preferences noted. If this relies on human memory, the experience design and execution might vary depending on which staff is on duty.

Technology supports humans where our capacity to recall, understand and sustain is limited; it helps us accomplish tasks better and more efficiently. The industrial revolution changed work by surpassing our limited abilities to produce goods with human hands. New technologies such as AI help us surpass our mental limits. AI will always need a human to support it, but by effectively leveraging it we can surpass our mental abilities in an unprecedented way, just as industrial machines helped us with our physical limitations.

THE MOVING TARGET OF CUSTOMER EXPECTATIONS

Customer experience work is never finished, mostly because of ever-changing customer behavior and expectations. What was sufficiently good for customers a year ago might not satisfy even their most basic needs today. Customer expectations are influenced primarily by the growing transparency and availability of information and the improvements in supporting technologies that impact businesses' ability to serve customers.

The customer constantly receives information about other customers' experiences from different channels and reflects them on her own expectations. One excellent experience surpassing the expectations of a customer sets a new starting level for the next one. Therefore, "overserving" a specific customer group may prevent a business from being able to maintain a sufficient service level as the customer expectations grow due to shared experiences. The customer will experience a disappointment even if previously the same experience provided satisfaction.

This is often the case with blog marketing. A blogger's experience at a hotel or restaurant does not necessarily represent the establishment's normal service. A customer visiting the hotel based on a blog review may be disappointed with an experience that differs from the one in the blog if, for example, the blog writer received better service than a "normal" customer.

And customers no longer have different standards for their banking, healthcare, or retail experiences. They expect the "best" experience across all sectors. We have similar expectations for a stay at a hospital as we do for a stay at a hotel, and the expectations for a school's online portal are similar to the best online games. The forerunners set new standards for customer expectations and these standards are evolving constantly.

The technology landscape is also changing rapidly. Big Tech players bring new innovations to the market one after another. Refocusing digital efforts toward changing customer expectations will help companies set the right tone for their digitalization agendas. Most companies are accelerating their shifts toward digital-first models faster than ever before. But the change should not be just about digitalization. It should be all about the customer and their changing needs, expectations and dreams.

2

TECHNOLOGIES AND
CUSTOMER EXPERIENCE

As consumers, a significantly growing number of our experiences involve one or more components of technology. Customers may have settled for technology's limitations in the past, but today the demand for technology-driven interactions, services, transparency and speed is increasing at an unprecedented pace.

The first flight to Mars, the first true algorithm for helping scientists better predict climate change with quantum computing–based models, a traffic system built for self-driving vehicles or a robot performing an open heart surgery may seem far off, but the vision, ambition and intelligence behind these initiatives will continue to drive technology innovations. The adopters will be those with an advanced digital customer experience strategy who constantly innovate on behalf of their customers.

Technology develops faster than most users will be able to learn how to use it. Yet individual users are faster than organizations, where significant effort is required when teaching the skills to adopt new working styles, communication channels and tools. This is due to the added process complexity and the need to bring most users aboard before gaining the full benefits.

From the customer experience perspective, the success is being delivered with simplicity: one swipe, one contact, one click. It is hard to make things simple. In the world of technology, simplicity usually translates into complexity. While we envision a car taking us to our desired destination with a simple voice command, there are some more practical topics to solve in the near future: How can a delivery company give an exact time of the delivery instead of asking a customer to be on standby from 8:18? How is a customer profile recognized at a store counter without the need for a piece of plastic? How is a person informed on what travel restrictions apply to them based on their Covid-19 history and vaccination status? These are the examples of our daily lives where old business models and tools still define the processes.

TECHNOLOGY RUNS THE WORLD

The pandemic showed us not only the importance of well-implemented technology but also its power when things around us change overnight. Nowadays it's all about the cloud. The concept of cloud computing has evolved from a "location for technology and infrastructure" to global platforms that enable companies of all sizes to modernize their

IT systems and refocus resources on customer-friendly applications and insights. The cloud has also given us a chance to serve customers in a personalized, data-driven way and to gain access to technology innovation like never before. The company data centers are no longer centers of data. Small businesses with the right technical talent, innovation and products can enter new markets and customer segments in a matter of days or weeks.

In late 2020, Gartner expected the global IT spend to grow 4 percent in 2021.[1] In July 2021, that forecast was updated to almost 9 percent! This means that, worldwide, we will have spent over $4 trillion USD during that year. IDC sees IT markets normally growing somewhat aligned with the GDP, but estimates IT spending to accelerate now 2x relative to the GDP.[2] An interesting detail on this calculation: within five to ten years, new technologies such as robotics, AI and AR/VR will also expand to represent over 25 percent of information and computer technology spending. That's a big shift to companies now using IT for simple productivity tools like email and conference calls.

In the coming years, the growth will mainly happen in four areas: cloud, big data and analytics, social, and mobile. While these technologies have been at the top of the agenda for many companies over the past several years, pressure to transform and innovate (or survive) and of course the pandemic are accelerating reprioritization of investments and technology deployments. Many companies have already made significant progress in modernizing their core systems by leveraging the global cloud platforms, automating processes, reshaping skills and unleashing developers and engineers to innovate with speed. Agility and optimization will lead to cost savings that will be invested in understanding the opportunities that these technology areas create.

In the future, technologies will be considered enablers. Any company on the digital transformation journey must understand its current state and its desired state without compromising the ability to leverage new technologies and capabilities for innovation, to bring new services and products to the market, to serve new customers and markets or to shape industry cost structures. Yet, as mentioned in chapter 1, true transformation is a sum of multiple key areas including corporate culture, processes and capabilities. *In the following years, the leaders of most, if not all, industries will be technology companies by their DNA.*

From Reactive Past to Predictive Future

Over the coming decades, the use of technology by companies that will win the race to provide the best experiences will be turned upside down with profound implications for every aspect of their business, from customer experience, to core operational processes, to the very nature of their products and services. To meet and exceed customer expectations without continuous input from customers, we have entered the predictive era, ushering out a decades-long, reactive past.

In the reactive past ("application first"), data flew "downward" from the applications that powered business in small drops or completely disappeared into the darkness of systems, organizations and silos (see figure 3). For the customer to gain a next level of service, a new form was required to be filled or a new number needed to be called.

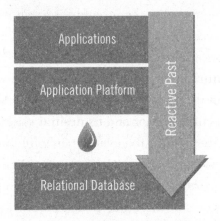

FIGURE 3

In the reactive past, data flew "downward."

Let's use the car industry as an example. A customer typically purchases a car from a dealer. One day the car stops running. The customer calls the service center and reports a problem. At that point, the service agent opens an application, types in notes about the problem and schedules a repair visit. That may be the first moment in years that any data related to that relationship has been noted, even if it was only a few kilobytes stored in a database and only in reaction to an event. And the manufacturer of the car may never see a single byte of the data.

This example can be seen across industries. Most enterprise and business applications are still no more than digital encapsulations of business processes used in the 1950s—not much more than pencil, paper and rooms full of filing cabinets. Nothing transformational there. And day-to-day, it is often the customer who needs to "integrate" between these applications and companies.

Today, the available technologies enable a different approach. A customer can purchase a car from a dealer. With appropriate permissions granted by the owner, the car provides a continuous stream of data back to the manufacturer and perhaps also to the dealer. The car may be self-driving and run a lot of data logic and computing power. It connects to the computer vision models in the cloud that are trained with the help of the data captured by sensors and cameras across the entire fleet. Every operating parameter of the engine, every press of the brake pedal, every trip route, every song listened to, even the risk factors of the driver profile provide a rich basis for prediction and can help maintain an ongoing and higher-value relationship between the owner, the dealer, the manufacturer and even those who provide additional services such as gas/electricity, repairs, insurance and financing.

This will be true for every vehicle, every thermostat, every piece of factory equipment, every social media update and every video call. Every single action on the planet is becoming a source of data and potential insight. This drives the fast-paced adoption of the Internet of Things (IoT) that is now enabled by the power, reach and connectivity of the global cloud infrastructures, faster data transmission speeds, lower latencies and more robust reliability offered by 5G and next-generation wireless technologies and a new arising theme of "Edge Computing." In Edge Computing, the technology platforms and innovation extend the core cloud and application technologies to vehicles, factories, robots, hospital floors and more to enable local processing of data for further automation, intelligence and action.

In the predictive era ("data first"), dataflows "upward," originating from every corner of the planet toward our customers' applications, products and services (see figure 4).

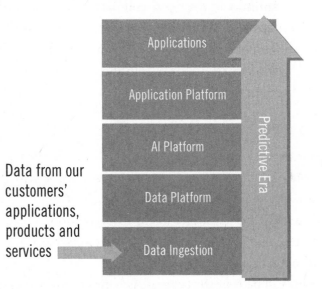

FIGURE 4

In the predictive era, data flows "upward."

From this data, impending failures can be predicted via an anomaly detection model and addressed proactively so that a driver is never left stranded on the side of the road. Better entertainment options can be suggested based on a driver's preferences and those of similar drivers across the customer base and better routing options offered by the navigation system based on citywide traffic patterns. Even the car itself can predict an impending accident, braking to avoid a collision. And the list goes on with endless possibilities. The car can connect with the identity of the driver to maintain repair histories, cost structures of fuel consumption, charging profiles or even complete payments with the energy company when connected to a charging station. All of this is possible if the supply chain in the back end is able to provide the expected outputs based on the data insights on time. This can be fully automated: the scarcest resource we have is time, which is what we can help the customer with! No more endless customer service loops!

And, of course, every data-driven, AI-powered action produces even more data, fueling a digital feedback loop of continuous learning and improvement. When we see a pattern, we can proactively get things fixed and avoid causing the same issue to other customers.

The enormous changes to come will reconfigure entire industries. The technology behind this is essential to address the needs of an "as a service" culture. Extending from our example, car ownership could become outdated. Manufacturers may become service providers; customers may become subscribers; and dealers may play an entirely different role in the reconfigured industry.

This is one example from one industry. But the opportunity exists across every industry, every customer and every business process. Leading in the predictive era requires most companies to broadly transform in fundamental ways. They have to transform digitally.

Customer Interface

In the predictive world, the automation and integration of back-end applications and providers coupled with constantly simplified user interfaces leads to less demand for the customer to provide data manually to complete their buying or service experience. For some companies, this means the need to reevaluate their supply chain and the role they want to play directly or indirectly in interacting with their customers. In the fashion industry, this has led several brands to return to providing a direct digital sales experience to their customers, bypassing the traditional reseller models. We discuss an interesting example of this in the retail industry section.

Traditionally, even IT companies have trusted different kinds of reseller and channel structures to ensure the sales of software and hardware to various customer segments. The power of the cloud and the as-a-service business model is not just about pushing new products to the market. It is essential in enabling new, centralized, fast-paced go-to-market models to drive innovation and services to the global markets. This is changing how these companies interact directly with their customers.

Connectivity in the digital world is a bare necessity both for the consumer and for any business. In the past, companies were focused on developing killer applications to justify the investments for higher bandwidths, more coverage, more expensive devices and next-generation mobile technologies. Now, when 5G is the next-generation mobile network technology being implemented, very few question the need for less latency and more speed, coverage and reliability. The big question in the industry is: who will eventually pay the cost of the infrastructure and who will be able to monetize it? And the work for defining 6G has started already.

Voice, speech, gestures, augmented or virtual reality, touch and robotics coupled with social media platforms, mobile technologies, connected devices and vehicles continue to shape the way customers can and will interact with digital services. This will continue to have a significant effect on all customer service. The ability to understand changes in customer behavior or preferences together with the agility to shape the product or service based on those insights is a key to success.

MODERN TECHNOLOGIES OFFER
ENDLESS OPPORTUNITIES

While for many companies, the core focus is to rethink the basics to prepare for the next decade of transformation and digital customer experience, the world of technology will be crowded with new innovations, buzzwords and visions (even now it's sometimes hard to keep up with all the new stuff). The emergence of the IoT is already contributing to significant market growth, and within five to ten years innovative technologies such as robotics, artificial intelligence, quantum computing and AR/VR will be the new normal. Enterprise applications will be required to manage internal and external core processes, but many of those need to be modernized to allow better agility, integration, dataflows and, most often, the ability to react quickly to changes in customer or market behavior.

The biggest challenge with new and emerging technologies will be finding (and keeping) the right talent. Especially in Europe, outsourcing (rather than building the core IT capabilities in-house) has dominated the enterprise IT strategies and operations in the past few decades. Many have stagnated, spending a significant portion of their technology budgets on maintaining the old environments with little or no ability to facilitate the experiments of any new technology innovations in practice. The rise of the cloud market has opened these doors in a different way. Yet, if the company has also outsourced its skills, it becomes complex to orchestrate. What happens when technology becomes an essential part of the business, such as designing the customer experience, the company's own IP, or its strategy for competitive advantage?

Companies that have adapted cloud technologies, acquired technical talent and modernized their environments are likelier to experiment with new technologies in advance and be ready to deploy new solutions when there is a wider market acceptance emerging. When we see availability improving, costs going down and required skills secured, we are ready to move forward. But will that be too late?

Artificial intelligence is one of the most invested-in and fastest developing technology areas. Yet its tangible outputs and concrete impact continue to be questioned. AI is imperative for the predictive era—for robotics, for streamlining experiences and for automating processes based on data and insights. AI requires skills in mathematics, statistics, data analysis, data models, programming, algorithms, frameworks, computing, machine learning—a long list. Therefore, the professionals are being hunted by the big technology companies and promising start-ups. The car example provided earlier already gives several instances where this technology area is required to provide the expected customer experience. Many Big Tech companies are luckily embedding this intelligence in their out-of-the-box software to be easily used (or at least more easily used). This requires constant software updates. With the current speed, tech gets old almost as fast as your bread from the bakery.

Augmented reality and virtual reality bridge the digital and physical worlds. They allow us to take in information and content visually, in the same way we take in the world. AR dramatically expands the ways our devices can help with everyday activities like searching for information, shopping and expressing ourselves. VR lets you to experience what it's like to go anywhere, from the front row of a concert to distant planets in outer space. Using the example of the car, in the case of a failure, the mechanic at the car repair service could create a digital 3D, AR model of the car indicating the point of failure, impact, needed repair plan and likely spare parts required. The same model could help this person to use the manufacturer-provided model as an overlay to the physical or the digital 3D model to quickly come up with a resolution for the problem.

Our ambition to provide technology-based solutions to solve the most critical and wicked problems of humanity, nature and our planet continues to push the limits of the current IT systems, which are based on trying to understand the world through zeros and ones. Hence the emergence of the research and development of quantum computing. Quantum computers perform calculations based on the probability of an object's state before it is measured instead of just ones or zeros. This means they have the potential to process exponentially more data compared to classical computers.

For example, a logistics company trying to optimize daily routes across fifty cities, or a financial business trying to balance its global investment portfolio, or a pharmaceutical company looking to simulate molecules to better understand drug interactions could all benefit from the advancement in quantum computing. The models required to understand the impact of global warming on nature, ecosystems and climate demand far more sophisticated ways to explore and understand the phenomena. And again, the largest cloud providers have already launched services for developers and researchers to try these technologies without the need to invest in such technology infrastructure by themselves.

DATA IS THE FUEL OF THE DIGITAL WORLD

No great customer experience is delivered without data. Data is the fuel of the digital world and oxygen for the digital customer experience. But trust can be lost quickly if the data or privacy is breached, identities are stolen, transparency is questioned, laws or regulations are broken, or data integrity is compromised.

As the technology advances, more ways of creating, collecting, storing, processing and managing data are becoming available. Quite often the company providing the service, product or experience owns, manages and secures the data. The laws and regulations concerning data sovereignty mandate or offer guidance about the roles of those who collect or process data. Many of the modern platforms and cloud services provide needed tools and technologies for people and businesses will remain to comply with these rules and regulations.

Yet, the regulations will continue to change and the responsibility will remain to ensure that the customer-related data, on all levels of detail, is protected and managed the right way. People are becoming more aware of the risks related to providing personal or behavioral data or data being collected without their direct consent, even if very few pay attention to the small print in the service agreements.

While is it important to ensure that the company has access to data that has a direct or indirect impact on a service or product offered, the threats of data misuse or even intentional criminal activities are rising. People with bad intentions are constantly seeking ways to exploit the systems and to gain access to customer data. It is no longer enough to secure access to the data. Businesses must ensure that the data is secured wherever that data may be collected, stored, processed or changed. Customers expect transparency and security. They expect their data to be secured from any misuse in any situation.

At the same time, customers expect ease of use. Most are unwilling to remember tens of user IDs and passwords. They expect their data to be shared with stakeholders, partners, ecosystem players and collaborators who provide any essential elements to the product or service. As an example, most of us expect our medical records to be available for anyone providing services critical to our wellbeing. It just remains unclear who is ultimately in charge of making sure that this happens. From the customer's point of view, unclarity means lack of trust.

The pandemic has pushed most companies and their employees to work remotely. This means that critical data is being accessed beyond the controls of the normal enterprise IT boundaries. Data might reside on remotely connected, unsecured devices, processed across non-secured connections, or managed on personal computers otherwise used for non-work-related purposes. Attacks to companies and government entities that store large quantities of customer data are becoming more sophisticated. Hence many are adapting a Zero Trust approach as part of their technology and digital strategy. Instead of assuming everything behind the corporate firewall is safe, the Zero Trust model assumes breaches and verifies each request as though it originates from an open network. Regardless of where the request originates or what resource it accesses, Zero Trust teaches us to "never trust, always verify." Every access request is fully authenticated, authorized and encrypted before granting access.

Laws and regulations cannot always keep up with the latest technologies and developments. They may be introduced only after the technology is already being implemented and used. But it is high on the agenda for lawmakers and regulators to best ensure customer safety, protection and rights. At the same time, the technology companies are asked to take a strong position to ensure that technologies are being implemented in a safe manner and not used for harmful or criminal activities. Security and trust are at the core of any digital customer experience strategy. That responsibility will extend to everyone in the digital world. Remember, you can ruin your reputation only once.

It's Not the Tech, It's the Value

The most important value of the vast cloud platforms and related ecosystems is the access to the modern technology without a need to invest in and implement all of its layers to deliver a digital experience. Companies with an ability to dive deep will invest in the lower levels of the technology platforms to fine-tune what is needed. That requires money and resources. Many will focus on software, data and applications at the higher levels that capture the essence of the company's value for its customers. Some companies will focus on collecting the best of the services, applications and transactional platforms, mainly to facilitate a continuous customer experience.

All of this requires technical skills and talent. Many times, this work is specific to the industry and the company's business. The next wave in the cloud market will be the rise of the industry clouds where platform providers and key industry players are coming together to create integrated environments on top of the common services to address the interface, communication, security, regulation, data integrity and application requirements for industries like financial services, retail, healthcare and automotive. New ecosystems and supply chains will be built around these concepts that further emphasize the need to solve some of the essential challenges in providing world-class yet secured customer experiences.

Developing IT systems and writing code is commonly considered a task for professional developers due to the complexity of programming, tools, and languages. While these skills are to be accelerated through new training and retraining programs, no-code/low-code platforms are now on the rise. The initiative is simple: enable (almost) everyone to become a developer. Through the advancement of these tools and underlying infrastructures, citizen developers can leverage graphical and visual tools to create applications to augment existing ones and related processes.

This means that people with less programming skills can quickly modify the ways to retrieve and analyze data and create simple applications among teams, organizations, business partners, core applications or, even better, at the front end where customers are being served. Following the logic, advanced digital services are built so that customers can "program" their service experience to their liking without disrupting the core of the service provided. Ultimate personalization is possible faster than ever before!

With all this, the amount of technically savvy customers will continue to grow fast and will not slow down as the new generations with advanced technical abilities are becoming the true consumers of the digital world. Making this a reality requires organizational cultures to be more open to experimenting and risk taking. True digital customer strategy needs transparency, data-centric decision making and innovation throughout the company.

3

LEADERSHIP AND
CUSTOMER EXPERIENCE

Most businesses have recognized the importance of the customer experience and, most importantly, the connection it has to the success of the business. According to Forrester Analytics Customer Experience Index, a one-point improvement in CX Index™ score leads to $8.51 annual incremental revenue per customer in banking, $8.22 in hotels and $5.23 in retail.[1] For the US retail industry alone, this translates to $523 million annually. The year of the pandemic showed us also that a laser-sharp focus on the customer helps businesses to sense changing customer behaviors and adjust to unexpected market changes.

The public sector has also begun to recognize the impact that better service and customer experience can have. The improved customer experience has led to enhanced access to basic services, better learning outcomes for students, more engagement and improved results for patients and a more timely, better overall experience for customers on digital platforms. Some projects have succeeded; some were not completed. All of them, however, have provided significant learning opportunities, and even one successful project can bring a notable competitive advantage, cost savings or improvements in customer engagement that lead to improved customer lifetime value and loyalty.

Developing the customer experience is not a single project with a start and end but a continuum that consists of various strategies, decisions and initiatives that aim for the same outcome. Ultimately this continuum forms a holistic change encompassing the unit or even the entire organization. Adding a chatbot on a website alone will probably not generate results but combined with redesigning the customer service processes for speed and proactivity and integrating different channels, the impact on the service the customers receive can be substantial.

In the 1980s, many businesses established quality organizations. "Quality" found its way into annual reports and statements. In the 2000s, the environment and social responsibility were on the agenda for most organizations. Both the work on quality and the environment were initially seen as stand-alone agendas: dedicated organizations were established and the projects were worked on by small, specialized teams. Occasionally the projects generated good results, but their total impact on the business was limited. Nowadays, quality standards are part of *all* work in business. The same is happening with environmental and social issues. The real change is only visible to the customer when the development work is part of everyday work and becomes part of the corporate culture.

This is true also for customer experience work: it cannot be assigned to a separate unit, but it has to be an integral part of everything the company undertakes.

LEADERS WITH PASSION WANTED

Even if 2020 will go down in history as a year of great change and upheaval, the pace of digitalization is not slowing down in the years to come: customer expectations, new players entering the market and technological innovations continue to evolve at an accelerating pace. This puts pressure on the customer experience work: its scope, strategic importance, required skills and right organizational culture. Previously there was more time to develop the customer experience and projects were more straightforward and clearly defined. Development of the customer experience has not always been a strategic undertaking and therefore it was given less time and attention on management team agendas and development budgets. Nowadays the customer experience is part of the strategy of almost every business.

With digitalization, developing the customer experience requires some new objectives. Customer expectations have increased primarily due to new standards and examples set by global competitors. Customers are also more aware of different options. They can easily compare experiences created by local and global players. And they can read about the experiences of other customers through portals, peer-review platforms and social media.

When starting to develop the customer experience, businesses should evaluate not just their boldness and ability to change, but also their skills and background in developing a digital customer experience (see figure 5). By examining these areas, a business can evaluate what its starting point is for successful development of the customer experience.

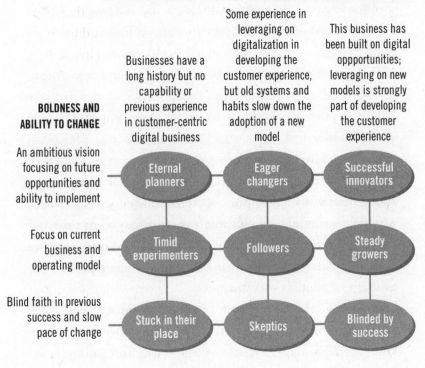

FIGURE 5
Developing the customer experience in the context of digitalization

Boldness and Ability to Change

When businesses evaluate the projects and objectives around developing the customer experience, they first need to consider their own ability to execute development projects and lead change. Digitalization is changing every sector. Management must be able to carry out change initiatives internally. Vision and strategy need to be well articulated and balance short-term results with long-term impact, and leadership needs to embrace change.

When businesses evaluate future development goals, they also need to take into consideration the systems that have been built along the way, the corporate culture and people's ability to change. Businesses that have succeeded in the digital age have cultures that encourage openness, cooperation, innovation, growth mindset and trust.

The pace of change is connected with the sector, and a unique product that is difficult to replace supports the business in the future as well. However, it is dangerous to rely on previous success and a product or service that is successful today. The best starting point for most businesses is a critical analysis of customer needs. Start the development work on this basis. It is not sufficient to evaluate the current state because digitalization is rapidly changing customer needs.

Boldness, agility and the ability to make changes become crucial if the external market conditions change drastically, such as during the Covid-19 pandemic. With everything changing in a matter of days, those that came out best managed to pivot their processes, resource allocation and even their offerings quickly. With a flood of customers coming to digital services, including many from totally new customer segments with different needs and journeys, a shift-change across the organization was required.

Skills and Experience in
Developing Digital Customer Experiences

Skills and experience have a major impact on the strategy for developing the customer experience: right talent is critical, but the organization also needs to rely on previous experiences. Skills and experience are bringing speed. Going through the learning curve takes time. If a company makes improvements with small steps, it is possible that in a couple of years the product or service will no longer meet the customer's need. Digital-first and digital-native companies have typically adopted an approach in which products and services are quickly launched and continuously improved by iterative cycles. Extensive trial and error accelerates learning. Sometimes it is better to make radical changes if the process is more strenuous and more demanding. Sometimes it is sufficient to have a long-term development plan set in stages.

If technology has previously been leveraged only to a narrow extent and it has mainly served the basic needs of the business (communication and enterprise resource planning solutions) or driven efficiencies and lowered operating costs (as opposed to improving the competitive position), the distance to catch up is longer than with a corporation that focuses on digital business as a starting point. Traditional retail banks, many of which have been using the same IT systems for decades, are leveraging digitalization. So are new entrants such as neobanks. This provides a good example of how the starting points, resources and culture of businesses that provide the same service can be very different. The same setting can be found in every sector.

ETHICS GUIDING YOUR DECISION MAKING

Ethics considers the right and the wrong; how humans (and machines) should act in different situations. What is "right" is strongly dependent on cultures, religions, communities and individuals themselves. There is always a lot of room for interpretation. Digitalization and evolving technologies, such as algorithms, increasingly require ethical choices from their owners and developers. Every business must consider how ethical values are transferred into everyday actions and decision making and which subsegments of digitalization require the most ethical attention.

And their decisions do not only define the future of the business, but of broader society. For example, how far do we want to go with medicine where there are limitless opportunities offered by quantum computing? If we could remove chronic diseases from every unborn child, would we do it? Or bring back a dead pet by cloning the DNA? Or determine the price of gas at the gas station by your license plate, based on where you live? Many things will be possible in the future, but time will tell how far we are willing to go.

Some future scenarios paint a threatening picture of robots and technology: soon we will be guided by algorithms, robots will take over our jobs and we will have to fight for humanity. In reality, technology and digitalization have for the most part advanced ethical themes. For example, supply chain transparency and trackability have improved with RFID-technology, and news of unwelcome operating models spreads quickly on social media and empowers other customers to bring them to the open.

Peer-to-peer platforms, such as Airbnb, Uber and Tinder, as well as marketplaces like Etsy and eBay, have enabled business based on trust between strangers. In a sharing economy, technology is changing how supply meets demand and creates the trust.

> Think about Uber. I came to New York in early '90s, when New York was as dangerous as any big city in America, when the murder-rate was seven times higher than it is now. And at the end of every evening, we would come together, pool our money and figure out a strategy for everyone to get home. If you had told me in 1993 in New York City that I could summon a car without making a phone call, without making any human interaction, driven by somebody I did not know or had never spoken to, which would show up unannounced and I would get in the back and it would take me without any conversation where I wanted to go, I would have said you were out of your mind!
> —MALCOLM GLADWELL,
> journalist and author, at 2021 Adobe Summit[2]

Previously many ethical decisions in day-to-day customer relationships were in the hands of humans, the employees. Going forward, technology will aid us in situations requiring ethical consideration. In the end, the decision will always be made by a human. Every business leader will need to be able to answer, or at least understand, ethical questions brought about by technology. On what grounds will an algorithm give an investment recommendation to a bank customer or a diagnosis to a patient? What will a self-driving car crash into within a situation where a collision has become unavoidable?

Will an algorithm treat all job seekers fairly or will it learn to favor young applicants, for example?

Ethical questions concern all corporate functions from ethical data gathering and handling to the impact their products have on human rights, the environment, society, the economy, working conditions, supply chains and the origin and safety of materials. In this chapter we will closely examine the ethical questions related to data and algorithms. As the amount of data increases and the threats related to it, such as cybersecurity and data privacy, become more common, businesses must carefully consider the ethical questions on gathering and using data. Also, the increasing influence algorithms have on decision making encourages an open debate and the establishment of commonly accepted standards for responsibility.

Gathering and Handling Data, Privacy Protection and Ethical Choices

In a digital era when data is emerging as the basis of competitive advantage and personalization for businesses, an increasing number of consumers are willing to give their personal data to businesses with the hope of having a better customer experience. This invites new ethical questions. How should the data be gathered and stored? What can it be used for and what possible biases can be caused intentionally or unintentionally? What ethical themes would it be good to have a discussion on?

- *Transparency of gathering, storing and handling data.* For many businesses that have adopted a "freemium" model, such as search engines and social media platforms, revenue is based on gathering and monetizing data from the customers.

Website and software End User License Agreements define the rights of the business and the customer. Studies have confirmed that consumers rarely read lengthy agreements and just click "accept." One of the most incredible news stories on this topic was about a test made by the cyber-security firm F-Secure in 2018. The terms for free Wi-Fi required users to give their firstborn child in return for access. A full 100 percent clicked "accept."

The General Data Protection Regulation (GDPR) in the European Union grants better protection to consumers' personal data and gives customers better means to control how their data is handled. Every customer has the right to access their personal data, gain information on how and for what purpose it is used, get incorrect information corrected and have their personal data erased and moved to another organization. How does your business handle customer data?

> If data is a new currency, do your customers understand the price they pay by giving their data? Is the "exchange rate" transparent?

- *The impact filters have on people's thoughts and opinions.* The election of Donald Trump as president of the United States and the information that Facebook used to filter the data presented to users has been discussed often. Social media's influence on people's opinions and their voting behavior is tremendous. Years later, US president Joe Biden is criticizing how the spread of Covid-19 misinformation and anti-vaccination content on social media is "killing people." What you read on social media is often selected and filtered; the platforms present stories and postings that have either been paid for or ones that you and/or your network have liked and shared.

Understanding filtering is one thing, but it is also almost impossible to know how many of the likes are from real people and how many are generated by fake accounts and algorithms. Distinguishing between right and wrong information has become practically impossible. Intelligent propaganda machines publish a formidable amount of fake news, and with the help of some technologies such as Lyrebird, anybody's voice can be copied. It is almost impossible to distinguish the real from the artificial. How can the benefits of technology be maximized while preventing its ethically suspicious use?

- *Profiling's impact on fair opportunities.* At best, profiling is the first step in personalization. It also helps the customer find products and services that suit their needs faster. Is profiling always fair and just? According to research by Northeastern University, it is not: the study shows that many platforms give different customers different prices based on their data, such as zip code, time spent at the website and browsing history.[3] Where do you draw the line between personalization and discrimination?

Artificial Intelligence, Algorithms and Ethics
As technology evolves, it is good for everyone to consider if artificial intelligence and the algorithms behind it have been

developed in the interests of the customer, the business, or society. Digitalization also forces consumers to be more critical: will a dating app find you the best possible spouse or does it hope that you will keep on searching (and paying for the use of the app)?

Technological development raises many questions that do not all have easy answers. The most important thing is to acknowledge the changes brought about by the development and actively search for answers on an individual, business and societal level.

- *Biases.* Algorithms are created by programmers. When developing them, the creators must understand both their own biases and the biases that are transferred to the algorithms. The importance of diversity has been promoted as one way to minimize biases among developers for a while now. But how to assess and mitigate algorithmic bias?

  With more investment going into AI-powered decision-making models, some companies such as Allied Irish Bank have begun to build algorithmic bias tools.[4] The tool allows users to evaluate if the models hold any bias or unfairness and it empowers AIB to continue to deliver fair, trustworthy banking to its customers.

- *"Right decisions."* In a tight spot, every human is capable of fast decision making. The decision is based on an assessment of the situation, but also on the individual's values. To a machine such as a self-driving car, all of this needs to be taught. But whose values and moral judgment should we teach the car?

MIT has developed a global Moral Machine that aims to gather people's ethical and moral values with regard to technology and AI.[5] The most widely used example is self-driving cars. Whose life should the car protect when fatalities are unavoidable—the passenger or a pedestrian? The passenger or a jaywalker? The passenger or a child crossing the street? The passenger or three pedestrians? Is the life of a working adult who contributes resources to society more valuable than an elderly person's? The conclusions of the Moral Machine vary by country and culture; there is consistency only about one thing: everyone hopes that the car will save the passenger's life if they are in the car, but also to protect pedestrians if they are not!

Even if some of the questions feel philosophical, they have to be solved when developing the technology. Self-driving cars will reduce traffic fatalities by up to 90 percent, but the decision about the unavoidable fatalities will have to be made. Germany was the first country to announce guidelines for ethical considerations related to self-driving cars. How can a business influence the legislation of its home country or country of operation? Can it actively participate in this kind of societal discussion and hence influence its circumstances?

■ *Solely for good.* Physicians are guided by the Hippocratic oath. Even if the oath is no longer actually taken in many countries, its spirit and a physician's commitment to ethics are a major part of a medical provider's professional identity. Many other professions also have widely accepted codes of conduct.

Cambridge Analytica's role in US presidential elections and how Volkswagen's programmers cheated in emission tests have contributed to the discussion about the need for programmers and others working with technology to agree on ethical guidelines. As there have been no global guidelines, many businesses have established their own. Almost every technology can be used for good or bad, and no ethical guidelines will be able to encompass every situation requiring ethical consideration. However, international guidelines would increase awareness, encourage open debate and guide the development in the right direction: to develop solutions that benefit the business, the customer and the society.

At best, algorithms help consumers make ethical choices, whether the question is about a product's origin, about human rights in a manufacturing facility or about a business's environmental impact. Machines can analyze a product or service provider's information efficiently and ensure that they meet the user's requirements. Imagine buying a new t-shirt and being able to see its full history: the field at which the cotton was grown, ethical practices in production, the type of transportation used, packaging materials and more.

Also, the possibility of human error is removed. A self-driving car, for example, will not pick up a cell phone dropped on the floor in the middle of driving and a robot surgeon's hand will not shake due to a party it had last night. But algorithms need to know how to deal with unforeseen circumstances. Businesses that develop these solutions will have to front-load the work on answering all the ethical questions.

"Microsoft Runs on Trust"

Businesses in the digital age are expected to be ethical, trustworthy, honest, just, and responsible when it pertains to their undertakings and decision making. The expectation to do "the right thing" often extends to the entire supply chain and ecosystem.

In addition to maintaining ethical guidelines, many businesses have begun to:

- Make ethics part of the organization's values and weave it into organizational culture.
- Measure digital trust.
- Increase transparency on how data is gathered, stored and used; the use of customer data should be fair to both parties.
- Benchmark ethical practices to other businesses in their sector and other sectors.
- Reduce ethical biases in product and service design by hiring diverse teams.

In the end, being ethical is part of a firm's image and brand. Many technology firms have made trust a part of their value proposition. For example, Microsoft says it "runs on trust." In addition to customer trust, a firm's ethical choices have an impact on its ability to attract talent; an increasing share of workers want to work for a firm that has a broader mission that is not just about economic productivity, but about improving the quality of life.

Achieving our mission all depends on building trust with people and organizations around the globe—our goals are only possible when people trust Microsoft and trust our technology.

—MICROSOFT

What happens when a company's ethics and integrity are on the line and its customers' trust is shaky? Google was in turmoil in early 2021 after firing both co-leaders of its AI ethics division over findings they made on the dangers of AI technology that is integral to Google's search products. The situation raised questions about ethical AI, research integrity, boundaries and ethical standards for technology. Time will tell what impact the incident will have on Google, but the company has tried its best with damage control—announcing a doubled head count for the AI ethics team and boosting the budget to evaluate any code or product to prevent harm, discrimination, and other AI-related challenges.[6]

According to Rachel Botsman, a leading expert and author on trust in the modern world, trust is a "confident relationship with the unknown." She claims that reputation is the most valuable asset businesses have and that trust is the currency of our new economy. Technology allows businesses to build trust with their customers in new ways, but one needs to remember that trust is something we have to earn continuously. It has to be a core value for a business and a core principle for product design.

Trust and adoption will go hand in hand for the next generation of products and services.

—ACCENTURE TECHNOLOGY VISION 2021 REPORT[7]

MEASURE WHAT YOU TREASURE

Traditionally, the customer experience has been measured with customer satisfaction scores and by using indicators measuring specific parts of the customer experience. In customer service, we have measured response times and lead times for processing possible reclamations; in production, it has been quality metrics and number of defects; in sales, the growth in customer accounts. It is easy to lose the big picture and ability to see the customer experience throughout the customer lifetime with the multitude of these indicators. And it is also typical for an organization to focus on a specific part of the customer experience (like the friendliness of the customer service) and treat all other phases and associated metrics as "nice-to-know." In the digital age, the customer experience does not always correlate with the picture painted by the selected stand-alone indicators.

Functioning and efficient processes alone are not enough. There needs to be real customer understanding, which is more difficult to measure than lead times. Along with company values, the customer-centric culture that provides guidelines for practical actions such as new customer-centric innovations, service concepts and everyday customer encounters should be measured.

Measuring the Customer Experience

The building blocks of a customer experience in the digital era were presented in chapter 1. We discussed four elements that every business should examine when developing a digital customer strategy: relevant offering, responsiveness, ease of use, and trust and continuity.

In addition to corporate culture, measuring should focus on these elements (see figure 6).

Measuring the customer experience in the digital age	
Customers are satisfied with our offering, and it caters to their personal needs	Customers think we are responsive and find answers and support fast
Customers think we are easy to engage with and we save their time	Customers trust us and think we can offer continuity and partnership
Our culture is customer focused	

FIGURE 6

The customer experience areas to measure

Traditionally, surveys have been the best way to measure customer experience. The challenge with surveys is their inaccuracy: often it would be more important to know the things the customers *do not* say. The results of one-off surveys also vary so much depending on the time of the study that it is difficult, if not impossible, to form a holistic view on whether the efforts have succeeded or not. All of us know that as customers our responses are influenced by many things other than the customer experience. Catching us at a bad time may lower our assessment of a positive experience. Also, our expectations impact our experiences: high expectations easily lead to bad overall experience even though other customers are giving high scores of the same services.

Going forward, businesses will determine the level of customer satisfaction by using different information sources. AI will help with this too. For example, in B2B sales, data analytics can be used to determine the state of the customer relationship by combining calendar- and email-generated information with modern customer relationship management systems. This makes it possible to look at the activity level of an account executive with different customers, for example. In B2B, sales activity has been shown to correlate with customer satisfaction. Mathematical models can be used to estimate the level of customer satisfaction when sales activity is combined with purchase data and the information obtained from digital channels by social listening.

Measuring a firm's digital presence cannot be overemphasized. Importance of social media in awareness, reputation management and customer service is growing constantly. Without tools for measuring and tracking social media, it is difficult for a business to identify defects, offer proactive customer service and increase awareness and findability. Information gathered from digital channels gives a good picture of how customers see a business or an organization quickly. Following trends and reacting to them without delay are especially important. The pace of change in the digital world is swift!

Culture and functioning processes ensure a good customer experience over the long term. A culture that emphasizes and cherishes the importance of customers is the most important starting point for building a customer experience in the digital-first world. Technologies that are used to help create the experience will in practice materialize the company's value proposition that reflects the culture. Technologies help not just the employees to achieve their best, but also the customer to engage with the business by using modern tools, channels and methods.

Customer-centric culture is not always easy to measure. It's often said that high employee satisfaction secures high customer satisfaction. The formula works both ways. Happy customers have a positive impact on the work environment, boosting customer-centricity and positive culture.

Invisible Technology Makes It Harder to Evaluate Experiences

Understanding, describing and evaluating the indicators measuring the customer experience used to be relatively straightforward. But with technology becoming invisible, value is created among several players in the ecosystem. With processes and systems integrating seamlessly, one should keep in mind that it has become challenging for the customer to evaluate things other than the end result! It is increasingly more difficult for the customer to navigate and understand how things are connected and how experience is created. When an ordered item does not arrive on time, should they contact the seller, the supplier or the distributor? At the end of the day, who is in charge of the customer experience?

The customer will also hopefully be positively surprised more often. "Wow, how did they do this?" Often the customer has no clue why or how the business has succeeded with its service proposition. It is difficult to give feedback on a world you do not understand. That is when the end result matters most. As with all measuring, it is important to evaluate whether the information obtained from the measuring is painting a correct picture of the situation experienced by the customer. Or has the business become lulled into false reality caused by irrelevant measures and incomplete data and a falsely fabricated picture while the customer is already searching for new alternatives?

Reviews Have Become an Increasingly Important Indicator

What should businesses measure then? There are three important customer experience metrics companies have used for quite some time now:

1. Net Promoter Score
2. Customer Satisfaction
3. Customer Effort Score

Net Promoter Score (NPS) is a good tool for evaluating willingness to recommend. There are many books on NPS where you can read more about its background and implementation. Willingness to recommend a company's product and services is still a valid indicator, but it's only one indicator. It reveals whether the customer was satisfied with the outcome of the customer interaction and is willing to share the positive experience with others.

Customer Satisfaction Score (CSAT) is the most popular tool to measure transactions. CSAT surveys ask customers to evaluate how satisfied they are with a recent interaction. These transactions are typically either purchases or customer service calls. CSAT is a flexible tool that can be easily customized with a simple rating scale.

We already explained how important convenience is in today's customer experiences. Customer Effort Score (CES) measures how easy the engagement was for the customer. A typical question could be, "Was it easy for you to find information about us?" CES is scored using a numeric scale. It is a customer service metric that is used to improve systems that may frustrate customers. It can help you to identify and remove the obstacles that are preventing your customers from engaging with you.

On top of the traditional ways to measure customer satisfaction, digital transformation has enabled other ways. Customer reviews have in many industries brought a new view to customer satisfaction. This direct feedback from customers can bring a lot of insights, but it can also expose companies to unfair criticism. Even if reviews have their own challenges, their power is undisputed, especially with sectors close to the consumer. For restaurants and hotels, reviews are a prerequisite; good reviews ensure customer flows. However, as a starting point for developing the business, the authenticity of reviews should be evaluated critically.

An interesting example of reviews and their risks is The Shed, which was listed as the best restaurant in London in 2017. The restaurant had a gorgeous website, an interesting menu, and most importantly, many reviews full of praise. Everything seemed perfect until it turned out that the restaurant did not exist.

The founder had asked his friends to post reviews on a virtual restaurant he had started as a joke. The experiment went so far that they actually opened The Shed for one night. The restaurant served frozen meals heated in a microwave oven and placed beautifully on a plate. The customer reviews continued to be excellent. No one dared to criticize a restaurant that had received so much praise and excellent reviews![8]

Digitalization sets new requirements for measuring the customer experience. There is a need for indicators that combine short- and long-term information into forecasting models where the state of the customer satisfaction and the true quality of the customer experience can be determined more reliably.

Like customer journeys, developing measurement is a journey. And just as customer journeys are varied, so is the approach and pace businesses need to take in developing the necessary capabilities and measuring them. Measuring customer experience in the digital, always-changing environment is far from easy. Wherever you are in your journey, we hope the examples from chapter 4 will inspire you and show that there is no right way to create digital or digitally powered experiences. The only wrong way to go about this is to do nothing and wait too long.

NO TIME TO WASTE

Where and when should one start? Surely this is something every business and organization considers in their development plans. We could try to seek an answer to this challenging question from one of the largest winners of the digital change. Apple's Steve Jobs said in 1997 that product development should start from the customer and consider everything else only after that. Jeff Bezos applied a similar leadership philosophy at Amazon since the start. He often mentions "customer obsession" and "laser focus on customers." The strategy and approach seem to be working. Apple's and Amazon's success stories are unrivaled.

A straightforward guideline could be to identify the customer's biggest pain points and solve them with technology. Things that frustrate the customer should be eliminated as soon as possible. Most of these issues are so ordinary to us that we rarely stop and think how things could be handled differently. Could you check into a hotel before arriving and get a code or a boarding pass like at the airport that would allow you to walk directly to your room? Why do you have to wait for the check for so long in a restaurant? Couldn't you just pay with the credit card you used when you made the booking, just like you can with Uber?

Customer experience projects that begin with the customer and are clearly defined usually succeed. Massive development projects that are impossible to lead and where the customer has disappeared somewhere in the wheels of bureaucracy do not. Developing the customer experience by leveraging technology takes courage and the ability to tolerate mistakes.

> I'm not a tech guy. I'm looking at the technology with the eyes of my customers, normal people's eyes. —JACK MA,
> cofounder and executive chairman of Alibaba Group

4

CUSTOMER EXPERIENCE
IN DIFFERENT INDUSTRIES

Each sector, business and organization views the customer experience through the lens of its own strategy, goals, resources and opportunities. Similarly, the role, the importance, the maturity and impact of digitalization vary sector to sector and business to business. Businesses often benchmark themselves against businesses in their own sector. But does it make sense for an airport to draw learnings on queue management from another airport, or, for example, from Disney World?

We believe that businesses have a lot to learn from one another across sector boundaries. The high-performing and innovation-intense businesses, regardless of their sector, are front-runners in applying artificial intelligence to automate operations and personalize experiences, empowering the service provider to have informed and value-added engagement, managing a holistic customer experience (beyond just their own business) or reimaging transparency in the supply chain. These topics are of interest to all sectors in one way or another!

Leveraging data effectively, embracing change and encouraging customer-centric innovation should be goals for all organizations. Developing partnerships, building ecosystems and leveraging platforms will help businesses to succeed when digitalization is shaking up various sectors. Developing the digital customer experience by focusing on real-time service, personalization and user-friendliness is something that touches upon all organizations regardless of their sector.

In the following chapters we will examine five sectors: retail, retail banking, travel and hospitality, healthcare, and education. At first glance they would all appear different when it comes to the customer experience:

- *Availability of customer data.* Apart from the number of passengers and destination information, airports do not have other customer information available. Customer segmentation and customer understanding need to be built through surveys. On the other hand, many schools have information on their students spanning several years, and hospitals have detailed individual health histories on their patients.

- *The role of the customer service provider.* In schools, the customer service provider (teacher) needs to provide an experience to twenty or thirty customers simultaneously. Physicians, on the other hand, tend to meet patients one-on-one. In retail and in aviation, the role of the customer service provider is lighter than in healthcare or education; retail salespeople and airport assistants have less impact on the holistic customer experience than teachers or physicians.

- *Amount of experience makers and impact of regulation.* At an airport there are often several dozen businesses and organizations that are part of building an experience that appears as a single experience to the customer, while in a retail store a service provider can manage all the elements of the customer experience at their will. Retail banking, airports and healthcare are more heavily regulated than other sectors.

- *Immediateness and impact of customer experience to bottom line.* Customer experience has a direct bottom-line impact for profit-seeking businesses, even in the short term. In public schools, a good customer experience will bear fruit in the distant future.

By examining the themes deeper, we can see that sectors share some surprising characteristics:

- *The length of the customer relationship.* In education and traditionally in banking, customer relationships span years, even decades. In hospitality, retail and aviation, customer relationships can be short. Generally, businesses seek ways of providing incentives to build long-term customer relationships. In which sectors are customer relationships getting longer? Which are facing shorter ones? What does this mean for the need to innovate and further engage customers?

- *Chain of experiences.* In healthcare and at airports, the customer experience is a chain of experiences provided by multiple operators. How do the different sectors manage the holistic customer experience? Who takes the lead on developing it?

- *The customer's sense of being in control.* In healthcare and at airports, one of the most important elements of the customer experience is the sense of being in control. Unlike in retail, a customer at a hospital or at an airport often feels that "someone else" is in control. What is the role of the customer in creating the experience? How much can the customer shape this experience?

- *The changing role of the customer service provider.* Digitalization changes the role of the customer service provider in almost every sector. Customers can get basic product and service information on their mobile phones or computers and then turn to the service providers for more complicated questions and support needs. In every sector, digitalization (data and efficient analysis tools) will enable the customer service provider to focus on the customer as an individual and provide more personalized service. How are companies empowering their employees, and how does the organization's culture need to change?

- *Competition in the customer interface.* For banking and retail, the competition in the customer interface is fierce: portals, aggregators and new entrants from completely different sectors are entering the market.

- *Customer expectations.* Customer expectations are becoming global and expanding over sector boundaries. The expectations regarding a stay in a hospital now share some of the same expectations as a stay in a hotel. A retail shop at an airport is expected to have as broad a selection of goods as its main branch, and expectations about an online learning portal are similar to expectations about online games. Where do your customers' expectations come from?

In this chapter, we will examine five different industries and what the customer experience means in each of these sectors. We will analyze the role of the customer, the importance of customer experience, how the experiences are created and the impact digitalization is having on the experience. We also include a case study highlighting the work of a customer-centric organization, its journey and its initiatives to improve customer experience.

- Retail provides amazing insights to those who seek to integrate online and physical experiences seamlessly.

- Retail banking as an industry is interesting to those who operate in a sector where regulations are currently changing the landscape completely and businesses need to find a new strategic direction and change their operating and earning models. Also, those that are challenged by defining their role as a customer-facing brand will find it interesting to read about the transformation in the retail banking sector.

- Hospitality has a lot to tell us about the power of portals and the impact of Covid-19 to the current and future business. In the travel and hospitality sectors, providing a memorable customer experience is part of the industry DNA, and a big part of the experience continues to be delivered face-to-face.

- Airports are the masters in orchestrating an experience across tens of different stakeholders with little customer data on hand.

- Healthcare offers insights into an operating environment that is highly regulated and includes a large number of privacy questions.

- Education offers a positive customer experience with important long-term goals and results. Typically, one experience serves several "customers" at the same time. How can one personalize it?

There is more amazing customer experience work happening around the world than we can include in this book. Above all, we hope that the examples we chose will give you new ideas and create conversation across sectors!

RETAIL

Retail is one of the sectors that has changed most rapidly over the past decade: the closer you are to the consumer, the faster digitalization happens. And consumers have changed their shopping behavior faster than retail businesses have digitized.

> The largest variable is not technology, but a consumer applying technology.

Globally, ecommerce grew in double digits in 2020. In the US, the growth was as high as 44 percent. From this, Amazon's share was almost a third.[1] The pandemic accelerated all things ecommerce and it remains to be seen if the change in purchasing behavior is permanent.[2] Adobe predicts that 2022 will be the first trillion-dollar year for ecommerce.[3]

The single largest change in retail happened when consumers began carrying shops with them, in their mobile devices. Previously, retail was strongly connected to a physical space and the retailer was able to control a customer's buying process inside the four walls. When shopping became more digitalized, the ability to control the process weakened for a while. The ability to change and adapt into a new kind of buying process combining physical and digital has separated the winners from the losers. The pace of change has surprised many and it will continue to be at least as rapid in the coming years.

Also, the growth of online portals and the power they have gained has surprised many. Amazon's technological advantage, customer experience on its platform, logistical efficiency and bargaining power in negotiations pushed many retailers that were struggling with digitalization into bankruptcy in the past twenty years. But a lot has happened since 1994 and the mass move of brands to a few big portals is now for the first time seeing a change. Nike decided to discontinue a collaboration with Amazon in 2019.[4] It wanted to build a direct dialogue and engagement with its customers and focus on its own sales channels. The move allows Nike to focus on strengthening its brand while better managing pricing, campaigns and discounts. It remains to be seen how many consumer brands make the same decisions. Success with this strategy requires a strong and well-known brand and investments to build sales channels. For smaller, less recognized brands, portals remain the most profitable option.

The key changes seen in the retail sector include:

- *From transactions to experiences.* Standard everyday transactions have turned into sales of products with services and experiences linked to them. Consumers are not buying products; they are buying experiences.

- *From scale to unique.* Previously, winners were businesses that were able to achieve an advantage by having large volumes. Now the winners are businesses that can best use data to personalize their products and services. Economies of scale do not always lead to success. Many consumers value environmental friendliness and ethical operations more than just a price.

- *From limited options to everything being available.* Previously, retailers controlled which products were offered to the customer. Retail was local and tied to stores. Now consumers define what they want and everything is always available (online) as a starting point.

- *From slow cycles to quick-to-market.* Product development was slow and new products came to market in a predefined cycle. In fashion, for example, it was twice a year. Now product development is continuous and businesses must be quick to react to trends. Zara has made its process so efficient that a product can go from a concept to the shelf in six weeks. The previous evaluation of historical customer data has turned to predicting customer trends. Businesses that are able to react to them can serve their customers best.

- *From controlling prices to full transparency.* Retail used to have significant power over pricing and it was difficult for consumers to compare prices. Now, competing on price is notable and the internet has made prices completely transparent.

From Many Channels to Seamless Experience

When retail began to digitalize, a large part of development projects focused on leading channels. Online and digital channels had their own development teams (still do in many organizations!) and the channels were seen as separate paths to purchase. Consumers were able to buy products online or at the store, but the transition between the channels was difficult, if not impossible. Often the product range and even the customer experience were completely different, almost as if you were dealing with a different firm.

It is difficult to talk about digitalization in retail without mentioning "showrooming." This means the tendency of customers to get familiar with products in a brick-and-mortar store but make the purchase elsewhere, online. Consumer surveys show that about a quarter of customers do "showrooming" and about half of them end up buying the product elsewhere. This phenomenon is expensive to retail firms if customers end up using another retailer online. Resisting selling online does not help, however, and the phenomenon can't be denied (some businesses have tried adding surcharges, with poor results). The only option to cope is to modernize and digitize brick-and-mortar stores.

Businesses and entrepreneurs also have to understand the connection between different channels in product pricing. For example, fashion retailers often sell their remaining stock online at the end of the season in international portals such as Farfetch. Products available in international online portals are often available in stores, but frustratingly the prices do not often match the ones online. An entrepreneur may think that the customer visiting the online portal is different from the one visiting the local brick-and-mortar store. Often the products in a store are priced higher than the ones in online campaigns.

However, it's quick and easy to try out the products at a store, then find a better price online and order the goods. When a customer purchases a product online, in addition to logistics costs, the seller needs to pay a commission to the portal. This means that the margin on the product would be larger if it was sold at the store at the same price or even with a slightly larger discount, which may entice the consumer to make a purchase decision at the store. Information availability, real-time data and integrated channels are starting points for a modern retailer.

The forerunners of digitalization have already moved from managing channels to developing the customer path and experience. This combines the different parts of the customer journey into one entity in which digital channels and physical encounters merge into a seamless experience.

The greatest misunderstanding in retail is that physical stores will cease to exist. Consumers love stores. Brick-and-mortar retail therapy is here to stay! Stores offer a place for people to meet and socialize and have different experiences. Shopping has a more important role in how people spend their free time than just purchasing goods. In the US, 79 percent of retail sales still take place at brick-and-mortar stores.[5] Even if the share of online purchases has grown year over year, the importance of brick-and-mortar is still high.

However, it has become more difficult to measure online vs. brick-and-mortar revenue as both shopping events include many digital and physical elements. When a customer orders a product online but picks it up at a store, which one should account for the revenue from the sale? With successful marketing and targeting, the business may be able to sell additional goods to the customer visiting the store. On the other hand, stores are digitalizing fast. At best, the customer may be able to order goods that are out of stock at the store directly to her home through a mobile app, even directly from the fitting room.

Previously, stores were designed to be impractical. This was an efficient strategy as it forced customers to spend more time in the store and shop for more items than they were necessarily planning to purchase. In order to find the product they were looking for, customers had to walk around the store and this is how they often ended up buying other stuff too. It's not a coincidence that special offers were way in the back of the store.

Today, only an impractical store will alienate customers. Customers have become more educated shoppers and they have often gone online beforehand to study what they would like to buy and what they wouldn't. The shopping experience must be pleasant, otherwise the customers will go somewhere else. There are always alternatives.

What should stores look like, then, and most importantly, what should they *feel* like? Customers should be offered a differentiated experience both online and in stores. Stores should be designed so that the different phases of the visit form a seamless experience. Products alone are not enough to differentiate; you also need to differentiate the experience. Department stores struggle with this fact. Online will always be a cheaper and more efficient way to shop. Hence the store should offer excellent customer experiences in addition to products. Coffee shops are popping up in even smaller stores, and offering a glass of champagne is not unheard of anymore.

Stores can also learn a lot from movie theatres! Even before the pandemic, many movie theatres faced challenges due to the increased popularity of Netflix and other streaming platforms. Why would you want to go to the movies when you can see the same films (including new releases) in the comfort and safety of your own home? The experience at the movies was expected to include premium services: something more to make it worthwhile, whether that was special reclining chairs, food and beverage services or nice bars to meet friends before and after the movie.

When customers no longer have to visit a retail store to get what they need, practical floor plans, lighting and music and other details play an increasingly important role. It is easy to stick with the new habits that we have learned during the pandemic: grocery delivery to your door sounds attractive in the future as well if the alternative is to go back queuing up at the cashier.

Digitalization has changed many things, but one thing has remained constant: the importance of staff. A poor recruitment policy, insufficient training and obsolete tools provide a sure path to failure. Customers expect more from service and service is the best way to create differentiated experiences for customers. Encounters with people leave the most sustained memories. Customers expect personalized service. A staff that knows you and your needs is a reason to return to the shop. Also, the expectation of a service at shops has increased: "Hello, let me know if I can help. We have more sizes in the back" is no longer sufficient. The customer expects expertise: in fashion they want to know about the designer, the materials, and the seasons. When buying appliances, the staff needs to know technical details but also new innovations and additional services. Many retailers have begun adding services such as installation, consultation, or personal advice.

The Purchasing Process at the Store Is Digitalizing

The purchasing process of the digital age differs from the time when customers used to just visit stores to buy things. In the first phase of digitalization, businesses started online stores side by side with brick-and-mortar stores. The outcome was often two completely separate channels between which customer information didn't flow efficiently, if at all.

A modern purchase process combines the physical and digital worlds into a seamless entity where the customer's needs and preferences are anticipated and answered with personalized messages and services. The outcome should be an experience that leaves a strong memory and ties the customer to the brand's value proposition.

1. *Starting online.* The majority of customers start the purchasing process online. The percentage share of this group continues to grow with new generations: generation Z already forms 40 percent of the population as of 2020. Customers search for alternatives and product information independently by using publicly available information and their networks. Social media and reviews play an increasing role.

2. *First interactions online.* Different kinds of profile-based recommendations, wish lists and personal service, such as chat, are the foundation of retail sales in the digital era. A customer is ready to disclose her personal profile and customer information if the business can provide her with personalized service. Seventy-seven percent of consumers trust chatbots to take down their names and addresses, while 76 percent say they trust them to help choose products.[6]

Customers want answers to their questions immediately. If the retailer is not able to provide the answer, customers look for it online and it becomes almost impossible for the business to control its truthfulness or tone.

Values, community and culture represented by the brand also have a large impact: in addition to personalized service, the customer expects a sense of community.

3. *Seamless transition from online to physical.* The purchase process that started online should transition smoothly to a brick-and-mortar store. The customer doesn't distinguish between channels; she wants the ease of searching online for products and the thrill of the brick-and-mortar store. At best the customer can be identified as soon as she arrives at the store and she can be provided with unique, personalized offers in real time.

    More than 80 percent of customers use a mobile device before making the final purchase decision at a store.[7] If the business doesn't provide additional information supporting the decision, the customer searches for it online, making it difficult for the business to influence the final decision. A customer visiting a store to pick up shoes she bought online can be offered shoe care products, insoles and other ancillary products at a discounted price. She can also be offered new products that are not available online yet or at all. This is what some fashion brands such as Valentino and Chanel do. This enables businesses to entice the customer to the store where the experience ties her to the brand. It also helps create an impression of exclusivity.

4. *Convenience through digitalization in the store.* There is one characteristic all modern retail consumers have in

common that is important to note in retail: they want convenience. The customer experience should be smooth and have no delays. The majority already think fitting is unpleasant. New technologies offer excellent solutions including a virtual fitting room where a customer can see how the piece she is considering would look on her without trying it on herself. Also, flexible purchase options, such as being able to take the products home, try them on there and return them to their chosen store if needed increase sales and improve the customer experience. The store needs to offer similar digital services that are available online: a convenient way to browse for available colors, how the product can be combined with other products, availability and so on. Stores will hence digitalize substantially.

5. *Expert staff.* Digitalization should also be reflected in the tools of the sales staff. Information is power; therefore, it should be available on the customer. Online, customers have become used to having access to detailed information on materials, the production process, color options and delivery times. The sales staff should have the same information in stores. However, it is still not uncommon to see staff making phone calls around the store in search of the right size for a product while other customers wait in the queue. This is not only frustrating for the customer waiting for the information, but it also delays the purchasing process for others. Real-time information systems and their integration are requirements for succeeding in retail.

As customers have access to more information than ever before, sales staff is expected to be more knowledgeable than in the past. In car dealerships, for example, some salespeople have been replaced by technical experts. Customers expect personalized and always available service from the start.

6. *Easy payment.* Surprisingly, the most challenging part of the retail customer experience is payment. Ever since Amazon launched its one-click purchase process, customers have ceased to be willing to queue, even at stores. It is easier to try the products at the store and buy them online. This also applies to groceries. Cash registers are slowly disappearing and retail needs to prepare for the next phase by testing and piloting different payment methods. The easier it is to make the payment, the more likely it is for the customer to reach a positive purchase decision.

    For example, Amazon GO already offers customers the ability to purchase products without being checked out by a cashier or using a self-checkout station. The products are charged on the customer's Amazon account automatically. It is also possible to make the payment a better experience by packing the products nicely or by having separate facilities, for example.

7. *Beyond the purchasing moment.* The purchasing process doesn't end with payment. It is important for businesses to review the customer experience as an entity, not just until the purchase decision. A couple of years ago, this

was still a challenge to many businesses, but now it is better understood. Especially online, where return percentages can be high at times, it is important to perform after-sales service with care. Also, presence in social media and supporting the purchasing decision are important. When, after making a purchase decision, the customer feels that she is part of a community or receives support for her decision, the return percentages decrease. This has a direct connection to profitability.

The most important areas of digitalization in retail are very similar to other sectors. Mobile technologies will play an increasing role. Also, among other things, identification based on location services and real-time campaigns improve communications targeted at customers at the right time. In addition to beacons, solutions for digitalizing stores include different kinds of digital screens and price tags, the previously mentioned self-checkouts and different kinds of mobile applications that use scannable QR codes. AI, IoT and virtual reality solutions will also be increasingly used in retail globally.

For example, pricing or updating pricing in a grocery store used to take several days. It was challenging to speed up the process even if there was a need to react to a change in availability or demand. Nowadays, updating prices for tens of thousands of products can be done in minutes, thanks to digital price tags. Price fluctuation common in the online world will become more common in stores as well.

The Environmental Impact of Online Retail

The huge growth seen recently in online retail and e-commerce has not only impacted the retail industry but has had a substantial impact on the broader society. Purchasing clothes online, for example, is so common now that it impacts the environment negatively. Clothing is the most popular product group in online retail sales, and the return rate is as high as 50 percent. The return rate for men's and children's clothing is significantly lower than for women's clothes.

Women like shopping and many still find retail therapy relaxing amidst their busy lives. In their retail euphoria, consumers also buy products they do not need or cannot afford. Continuously improving user interfaces and effortless payments entice consumers to easy purchase decisions. Just "One Click" and you have bought the product already.

However, returns are an increasing problem for two reasons. First, they increase logistics costs, which need to be compensated for by increasing prices or reducing margin. Second, they have a significant environmental impact. The global fashion ecommerce industry was worth almost $500 billion in 2020. We saw some decline from the previous year due to the pandemic, but the market is set to recover up to almost $700 billion in 2023.[8] In the world's oceans there is constantly a huge number of packages sailing back and forth between shops and homes. Some of the clothes are not even planned to be worn. It is easier for the consumer to order a couple of different sizes, keep the right one and return the others.

With the predicted growth of online retail sales, consumer behavior needs to change in order to reduce (preferably minimize) the environmental impact. This is challenging as consumers have already become used to free deliveries and returns. It is already difficult for small online retailers to compete with the giants because the large operators offer excellent delivery terms. Weaker terms would probably slow down the business for the smaller ones. Therefore, the big ones will have to lead the way.

The first steps in the right direction can already be seen. Amazon has announced that it will remove customer accounts and "penalize" customers who abuse the free delivery service and return products excessively. This not only improves the firm's profitability, but also guides consumers toward more environmentally friendly behavior. On the other hand, Amazon has received a lot of bad publicity because it destroys millions of returned products that are functioning well and arguably brand new.[9]

In addition to the change in consumer behavior, new technologies also help decrease the number of returns. In clothing, the most important aspect is finding the right size. Standardizing sizes with clothing manufacturers is slow and difficult. But when a customer has the ability to scan her body and try on clothes virtually, it helps reduce the number of returns significantly. It is also essential to combine physical and digital shopping environments and entice customers back to stores by offering experiences and services. When a customer tries the product on at the store, the risk of return is reduced even if the actual sale takes place online.

CASE: Alibaba

When discussing digitalization in retail, it is impossible not to touch upon two firms: Amazon, which started by selling books online, and Alibaba, which has been an incredible success story in China. Amazon has been used as a case study in many management books, so we will examine Alibaba, founded by Jack Ma. Digitalization is highly advanced in Asia and new services are constantly launched to serve a growing and increasingly wealthy customer base.

Launched in 1999, Alibaba is currently number seven on the list of the world's ten most valuable global brands.[10] In addition to the successful online shop, Alibaba.com, Alibaba's businesses include Taobao.com, which focuses on trading between customers. The revenues from ads on Taobao are the second largest revenue stream in the group after Alibaba.com. Alibaba also offers digital payments and cloud services like its competitor Amazon (through Amazon Web Services).

Alibaba currently has business activities in two hundred countries. Since 2015, its online sales have exceeded the combined sales of all online retailers in the US! The figures include real giants such as Amazon, eBay and Walmart. Sales outside China have been relatively small, but it remains to be seen how aggressively Alibaba will seek to increase its global market share. The company has shown steady growth outside the home market where it is dominant.[11]

Alibaba Reformed Grocery Stores into Oases of Experiences

In addition to developing online sales, Alibaba has boldly begun to reform China's retail sector. For example, Alibaba has entirely reformed grocery stores. Its latest concept is "Hema," a store that delivers food and groceries within a two-mile distance in thirty minutes. Hema is so popular that people are deciding where they want to live based on the distance to the closest Hema! The Hema stores are oases of experiences. Their diverse offerings include handpicking shellfish directly from a tank and requesting a chef to prepare a meal of it while you wait. You can have the meal at the store or to go.

Hema is a perfect example of a new shopping experience combining online and offline where a purchase process guided by data and mobile devices is continuous and effortless. A customer downloads a mobile app through which she receives information on every product at the store by scanning. The app recommends products based on the customer profile and previous purchases. People often forget stuff when shopping, but at Hema the app reminds you about the missing milk. And if you are too tired to go to the store, you can do your shopping online and have it delivered to your home. When you check out (Hema has no cash registers where you load every single item onto a conveyor belt), you show the app to the cash register and the payment can be processed with an Alipay account integrated to the mobile app.

Reimaging the Customer Journeys

Alibaba has also sought to renew how Chinese consumers buy cars. Its auto vending machine has been designed purely with the customer in mind. Traditionally, customers had to visit each car dealer separately when they wanted to test-drive cars. Previously, booking a test-drive always required having a conversation with the dealer. Alibaba's new concept brings different cars to one location for test-drives. Customers can select the cars from a mobile app and after the test-drive they can even buy the car using mobile pay. This is very simple and takes about ten minutes.

In 2018, Alibaba announced a partnership with Ford and is now expanding the concept to cover other brands.[12] The vending machine is five stories tall and holds forty-two cars. Customers log into the Alibaba mobile app with facial recognition. When the customer arrives at the vending machine, she is identified again and the machine brings her the desired car. There are a few requirements. Customers need to have a high score on their Alibaba Tmall accounts to be able to use the service.[13]

Alibaba has also tested other ways to sell cars. In 2016, it organized a sales campaign online that resulted in selling one hundred new Maseratis in a few seconds. In addition to a successful business outcome, the most important value of these pilots and campaigns for the company has been the constant innovation to improve customer experience. The skeptics could claim that we are still buying cars the old-fashioned way (even in China) and the expansion of the concept wasn't as fast as planned. There are always challenges coming with the new business models, and not all of them are successful. But these trials are integral to checking the customer pulse, to test new ideas and to adapt them quickly.

Everything That Can Be Digitalized Will Be Digitalized

Along with its other innovative activities, Alibaba has digitalized traditional corner shops and minimarts in China. Among other things, it offers the corner shops a light Enterprise Resource Planning app that enables the shops to monitor customer information and place orders (naturally only from one supplier, Alibaba).

Modernizing the shops doesn't only mean technology. They have been branded in a way that makes it easy for consumers to identify where new, digital services are available. These shops are most likely to have the goods the consumer is looking for. After all, the shop has ordered its merchandise based on customers' purchase data and fast-changing consumer trends. A product may become extremely popular on social media in a couple of days and of course the consumer wants that specific brand.

Alibaba has boldly embraced the challenge of digitalizing entire shopping malls: it doesn't believe that malls will be deserted, not as long as modernization is done right and on time. In Alibaba's model, many new digital services have been used to enrich the shopping experience. The stores use facial recognition technology to monitor customer behavior, among other things. For example, Alibaba offers targeted discounts on products around which the customer has smiled or for which she has previously searched online.

A customer no longer needs to carry her shopping bags around. She can leave the goods at the store for Alibaba to deliver (guaranteed in three hours). Thanks to integrating facial recognition and customer information, the customer doesn't need to provide additional information; the address information on the customer profile can also be accessed by the store. This sounds simple, but it is not yet possible at many other places.

In addition to combining traditional and online sales, Alibaba has digitalized the women's restrooms at the shopping mall. The company noticed that women spend a surprisingly long time in the restroom, regrettably often waiting for a free stall. So it installed screens in the restrooms, enabling customers waiting for their turn to try on products such as lipstick virtually, then snap a picture. The screens use radio-frequency identification (RFID) and AR technologies. The lipstick can conveniently be bought from a vending machine using the screen.[14]

Alibaba believes strongly that shopping is increasingly more entertainment (retailtainment), especially for millennials. Shopping should be interactive and game-like. The new generation of consumers is digitally native and doesn't want to just put products in a basket when they shop online or at the store.

In 2021, Alibaba's greatest annual sales event, Singles Day, generated sales of $85 billion.[15] This was double the sales in 2019! The main attraction of the event was an online fashion show, where big brands presented their products. Instead of just watching passively, consumers were able to buy the products immediately. A virtual fitting room enabled customers to "fit" the clothes once they had entered their height and weight. It was also possible to add accessories such as a watch or lipstick to the virtual fitting.

Alibaba also uses gamification in its strategy. By playing online games, a customer can get better discounts. Alibaba's game works on the same principle as the popular *Pokémon Go*. But instead of small creatures, the customer chases discount coupons that they can use when visiting a store. Of course, the same coupons can also be used online.

RETAIL BANKING

Banks are museums of technology.   —ANTONY JENKINS,
Executive Chairman, 10x Future Technologies
and former CEO of Barclays Bank

Many traditional banks were founded before computers were invented, so it is not unheard of for banks to have systems and applications from every decade starting from the 1960s. These technologies, from mainframe computers to ATMs, from online banks to mobile apps, have answered the needs of each era. One system after another has been added to the banks' IT portfolios.

The potential for cloud technologies, AI and machine learning to revolutionize the banking sector is tremendous; automating customer service, efficient use of data in credit risk analysis, distributed ledger technology and cryptocurrencies are commonplace and will become mainstream in the coming years. Banks have been slow to leverage new technologies, the cloud, data, AI and Application Programming Interfaces (APIs), but the impact of these technologies to the sector was recognized well before the pandemic. By 2016, 81 percent of banking CEOs said they were concerned about the speed of technological change, more than any other sector.[16]

Open banking regulations have accelerated the change. The Payment Services Directive (PSD2) in Europe forced banks to open their payment and customer interfaces to third parties. The new payment directive also increased the opportunities to offer innovative and friction-free services and new alternatives to customers. Open banking will enable "banking as a service" where banking happens via an app that customers can delete and replace, even with an app from another bank. Already today, at BBVA, a Spanish bank, non-customers can use their bank's app via open banking.

New entrants keen to enter the financial services market are often Big Tech firms such as Amazon, which already offers financing through its Amazon Lending service. With Amazon Cash, consumers can deposit money in their Amazon accounts at more than ten thousand retailers. Big Tech firms have digital capabilities, a wide customer base and an ability to build data-fueled and hyper-personalized experiences in real time.

Big Tech firms are riding high on customer confidence and trust in their brands. According to a study by Bain & Company (133,171 banking clients in twenty-two countries), customers in the US and the UK would be equally likely to trust Amazon and PayPal to manage their money as banks overall.[17] The tech firms are most keen to expand into financial services in countries where most business needs to be handled in a bank branch and where it is difficult: in India and Mexico, more than 80 percent of consumers would be willing to handle their banking needs with Big Tech firms.

Also, completely different new businesses find the financial market interesting: Starbucks, known for its coffee shops, has more than $1.2 billion on its loyalty program accounts—more than many banks![18] In the Nordics, IKEA (furniture), Norwegian (airline) and Schibsted (media) also offer financial services. In China, Alibaba's daughter company Ant Group offers payment and other financial services to more than seven hundred million consumers and has a larger market capitalization than Goldman Sachs!

Ant Group sought an initial public offering (IPO) in November 2020. Just two days before the IPO, the Chinese regulators extraordinarily suspended the process and decided to redefine Ant as a bank. What probably drove the decision is the realization that Ant had become systematically important. Despite the fact that Ant had announced in its IPO prospectus that "Ant Group is not a financial institution" it is now regulated like one. This demonstrates how the borderline between banks and other operators in financial services (fintech) is not clearly defined.

Digital innovations together with changing regulations and consumer preferences are shaking banking to its core: banks face competitive threats simultaneously from multiple directions. And as with all the other sectors, Covid-19 has accelerated the change faster than imagined: changes in consumer behavior have skyrocketed the adoption of digital banking services.

As new entrants are conquering the customer interface and offering fast and innovative services, banks are left to consider their role and business model in the changing world. Will they remain consumer brands or take a step back and become providers of the backbone systems? Will banks be needed at all going forward? Can we imagine a future entirely without the banking sector? What is also interesting is how the entrants offer services for free that traditional banks charge for. In a world of shrinking margins for fees and near zero interest rates, can banks identify opportunities for revenue while retaining customers?

From Bank Branches to Mobile

A bank's mission is to serve the customer, solve their problems, and perhaps even foresee and prevent future problems. A couple of decades ago, a customer experience with a bank occurred at the bank branch. At the time, developing the customer experience meant improving the service at the branch: programs focused on enhancing the branch environment and offering incentives to branch staff.

In 2012–2013, there was a major shift in the way large international banks approached their customers: with the lead of Citibank, one by one the banks removed sales bonuses for their branch staff. Staff was rewarded based solely on customer satisfaction, not on selling additional services. A customer was no longer considered a potential sales target for a product or a service, but a consumer to be served. The banks shifted from maintaining the customer relationship to managing it.

Even before the pandemic, many banking customers felt that visiting the branch was unnecessary, even annoying. They wanted to pay their bills and move money flexibly, the way they handled other things in life. Mobile was fast becoming the main channel for the customers' banking needs. According to Bain & Company, in 2017, mobile was the most used banking channel in thirteen of twenty-two countries and about 30 percent of banking globally was handled via mobile.[19] As a result of the pandemic, the shift to digital has been drastic: for example, in the United Kingdom, NatWest Group experienced more than 500,000 new mobile app downloads and 485,000 new online banking customers in the first half of 2020.[20] TSB, a mid-sized retail bank in the UK, reports that 89 percent of customer transactions are now being completed digitally.[21] And by 2024, mobile banking will outpace physical branches in the UK![22] According to PYMENTS Digital First Banking report, in the US, 89 percent of bank customers use mobile banking apps to manage their accounts.[23]

Mobile banking going mainstream is an Uber-moment for the banking industry. Technology has changed a sector to make things significantly easier and better for the customer. Other recent Uber-moments include contactless payments, which is drastically changing the usage of cash and cryptocurrencies.

From Lifetime Relationship to Experience Hunting

Before, customers used to be loyal to their bank. An account opened in childhood led to a lifelong banking relationship that was cherished despite changes in circumstances. Nowadays, changing banks many times has become a norm in our lives. Increasingly the reasons for switching banks include the quality of the customer service and the customer experience.

It is also quite common to buy products and services from multiple providers: over a third of consumers have purchased a product from a competitor of their main bank. The most common services that are purchased outside the main bank include wealth management and foreign exchange. The other providers have been able to generate a better customer experience for these services than traditional banks.

Digitally native consumers especially will diversify their wealth management and banking to several businesses. According to a report by Capgemini and European Financial Management Association, almost half of Generation Z customers are frustrated with the narrow range of products and services offered by their traditional bank.[24] They are happy to bank with players that offer services that match their preferences and work with the other services and applications they use. They are not interested in complex product portfolios, but want to see simple, transparent offerings with customer-friendly packages.

> Millennials are more loyal to the last good customer experience than to any particular (banking) institution.

Increased economic uncertainty, job losses and changing circumstances during Covid-19 have created a demand for more financial tools and guidance.[25] The value of financial planning is increasing. Digital-only banks, such as Monzo and Starling, are well positioned to tap into the demand by offering value-added insights, from spending analyses to changing utilities providers to helping customers to better control their spending. Already before the pandemic, these neobanks were successful by understanding the challenges and ambitions their customers had during their life journey (customer-first mindset), improving financial health and wellbeing of their customers and designing digital products to address a variety of financial pain points while having meaningful interactions with them.

That customer-centricity, right and innovative product offering, sleek customer experience and strong focus on transparency, community and customer satisfaction have attracted almost forty million customers to bank with neobanks![26]

Between 2010 and 2020, we witnessed the birth of more than 300 neobanks and challenger banks.[27] A trend that has not gone unnoticed by executives of traditional banks: 25 percent of them said that they worried about competition from their peers (other traditional banks).[28] And 66 percent saw neobanks and challenger banks as a threat.[29]

Are Banks Becoming Data Platforms?

As with other sectors, customer-centricity must be the common thread guiding the business, and all the employees need to strive to improve the customer experience. The experience must be seamless: the organization and the systems need to function together. Digital transformation should be embraced; it should be seen as an opportunity to reach customers in new ways and allow more informed and personalized service in face-to-face service situations. Planning and operations should revolve around the customer and her data, not around products in the bank's portfolio.

Data Is Oxygen

One of a bank's main assets is data. Banks possess a huge volume of data on their customers: their income, expenses, goods they buy, their creditworthiness, risk tolerance and more. Governing this data is at the core of banking. Unfortunately, this huge volume of data is often fragmented across various systems and databases that have been developed one by one over the past decades. Managing the data is therefore expensive and using it effectively is impossible. In the 2021 FSI Trends Report, 53 percent of banking executives said that modernizing core legacy systems is their number one priority.[30] Also, according to some studies, up to 70 percent of banks' IT budgets are spent on maintaining existing systems and only a fraction can be allocated to innovation.

Technologies such as AI and experiences that are personalized are all based on data. Data is vital! It is needed for the services to be effective and to ensure that the customers receive the promised benefits. Up to 67 percent of consumers are willing to share even more data with their banks in exchange for new benefits, such as lower pricing on products and services.[31] These customers assume that their data is used for providing personalized advice and offering the kind of benefits and products that fit with their life situation, goals and needs.

From the customer's perspective, the one who manages their data so that it will be beneficial to them is the one they want to do business with. Customers want to feel that they understand their monetary affairs, are getting a good deal, are in change of their own finances and have a supportive financial service provider.

Data, technologies and the customer experience have traditionally belonged to one organization (see figure 7). The bank had the information, which it processed and managed to create the customer experience.

FIGURE 7
Data is vital to the efficient use of technology.

In the future, the process will no longer be governed by one organization. When data and assets have been distributed and can be accessed by third parties at the customer's discretion, the winners will be businesses that can create a meaningful, valuable, context-related and personalized experience based on the data. New technologies, such as the distributed ledger, are pushing banks and their centralized databases away from their traditional role in maintaining up-to-date books on each customer's assets. In a distributed system such as blockchain, the information sits on countless computers.

Automation—Faster Speed

Customers are increasingly willing to receive more automated, system-generated support and they have grown accustomed to it. What is driving the increased willingness is cost efficiency, consistent quality and reliability of service. In the future, an increasing share of banking services and recommendations will be generated with the help of computers. For some customers it is already the only service experience at a bank, even with complex issues and products. Currently, 71 percent of consumers say they would be willing to move to a completely technology-assisted banking service.[32] Robo-advisors, chatbots, and virtual assistants have mushroomed across the digital platforms.[33] Santander Bank in the UK noticed that live chat and chatbot use was sixteen times higher in July 2020 than in January of that year. HSBC reported ten million chat conversations in 2019 and expects to reach ten million *per month* by 2024.

While we may need a few more years for AI and data analytics to evolve to ensure the chatbots can handle more complex financial tasks, they will play a key role in serving banking customers better in the near future. "Conversational banking" (interacting with a machine to discuss your finances) appears on almost every bank's digital strategy, and while the idea of obtaining a mortgage over the internet without human interaction still seems a bit awkward, we are not far from a time when an AI-based system will not only gather and store all digitally available information on our education, lifestyle, employment history, credit history, risk tolerance and financial situation, but also propose a next best action on the relevant products (such as mortgages) that the customer may be interested in. The mortgage itself will be signed digitally and the shares in the housing cooperative will be transferred on a blockchain.

Automation also enables banks to anticipate problems and recommend proactive steps before a potentially poor customer experience. For example, when the customer leaves for a vacation, the bank is aware of the destination and will not automatically close her credit card when it has been used abroad. These kinds of simple solutions are easy to implement with the help of machine learning.

From Competitors to Partners

Antony Jenkins, the former CEO of Barclays Bank, has said that the cooperation with a traditional bank and a fintech start-up is "like an elephant and mouse dancing." They have completely different perspectives. One side has vast information systems while the other has flexible, targeted and flashy apps based on the latest technology.

At a traditional bank the organizational structure is huge and the culture is based on risk aversion and minimizing change. Fintech firms, on the other hand, have agile, innovative, fast-moving teams. Traditional banks have the advantage of experience and the ability to navigate regulation. Their budgets and resources are often vast and their customer bases wide (for the time being).

In an ideal world, one would combine the best skill sets and resources from both sides. But finding a song that both parties would like to dance to might take a bit longer. According to the World FinTech Report 2020, 70 percent of fintech firms struggle to align culturally or organizationally with their bank partner and only 6 percent of banks say they have achieved the desired ROI from a collaboration with a fintech firm.[34]

A significant part of today's banking business involves the formation of new kinds of partnerships and the building of a new kind of ecosystem. According to World Retail Banking Report 2017, 91 percent of banks and 75 percent of fintech firms believe that cooperation in the future is likely. In 2020, the World Fintech Report stated that traditional banks must embrace Open X or they will become irrelevant. A year of pandemic later, World Retail Banking Report 2021 confirmed that the pandemic catalyzed the need for digital experiences and transformed the ideas and vision of open-platform banking into reality.

The future success of banks depends on adopting a more open model, which means opening and leveraging the APIs: open architecture banking enables managing payments, investments, loyalty programs and accounts in new services such as online retailers and social media. Culturally, the question is about promoting and supporting partnerships and ecosystem thinking.

The collaboration enables the development of innovative services and experiences, which will speed the development of a holistic banking experience. Simply put, it will offer more choice to the customers, such as the ability to bank where they spend and socialize. Customers are ready for this. The use of open banking doubled between January and September 2020 in the UK.[35] More than two million consumers use aggregation apps every month to gain better insights into their finances.[36]

While most API development at banks is still focused on internal API work aimed at eliminating silos and enabling smooth operations, there are already a number of excellent examples of innovative responses to customers' expectations on the market. For example, Bank of America's customers can perform transactions through Zelle—a peer-to-peer payment service allowing customers to send, receive and request money via mobile. Barclays's customers can receive digital receipts through a partnership with Flux; in Belgium, ING allows its customers to manage their subscription services through ING's digital channel, thanks to Minna Technologies.

At its best, the banking sector of the future will be a flexible ecosystem based on cooperation, spreading across traditional industry boundaries and offering customers cohesive experiences. Integration, APIs and leveraging customer data will enable personalized, proactive, automated services. World Retail Banking Report 2021 call this "Banking 4.X," which is built on harvesting data on customer behavior to hyper-personalize interaction. In Banking 4.X, banks become enablers and finance is invisibly embedded in the customer's lifestyle.

> Banking 4.X—a boundary-bustling era in
> which banking is embedded into customers'
> lifetime experiences and made invisible.

CASE: Virgin Money

Offering everything from current and savings accounts to
mortgages, yes, Virgin Money is a bank. But don't worry, we
never act like one.   **—VIRGIN MONEY**

The global financial crisis decreased consumers' alternatives
in the banking sector, and the UK was not spared from this.
After the crisis dissipated, in 2011, the three largest banks
managed 75 percent of all bank accounts in the country. This
situation was seen as risky. If another crisis were to occur, it
could lead to new, extensive government guarantees. Therefore, there was a strong drive to support the next generation
of smaller players.

Changes in regulation did bring about new players on the
high street, on the internet and on mobile. Metro Bank ap-
peared as an independent brick-and-mortar bank and TSB
found a niche by detaching itself from Lloyds Banking Group.
Virgin Money established itself as a challenger bank.

Virgin Money had launched in the UK in 1995 with the
name Virgin Direct. It changed its name to Virgin Money in
2000 and obtained a banking license when it acquired
Church House Trust in 2010. At first the business focused
only on credit cards and insurance.

Its product portfolio and customer base widened substantially in 2012 when Virgin Money acquired Northern Rock, a British bank. Along with the deal, Virgin Money acquired seventy-five branches, a million customers and savings account and mortgage-lending businesses. With the addition of savings accounts, Virgin Money became a retail bank. The current Virgin Money company was formed after Clydesdale and Yorkshire Bank Group (CYBG) acquired the smaller Virgin Money business in 2018 and adopted its name.

Today, Virgin Money has 6.5 million customers in the UK and it is the UK's sixth largest bank. It offers mortgages, savings accounts, credit cards and various investment and insurance products. Virgin Money positions itself between the major banks and neobanks bringing together a strong innovative brand and a customer-focused, lifestyle-driven proposition with strong digital capability and open banking (see figure 8).

Disrupting the status quo

Strengths of a major bank	Better than both MONEY	Strengths of a neobank
Primary relationships		Innovative brand and edge
Trusted brand, loyal customers		Customer lifestyle intelligence
Full personal and business offering		"Pay and play" functionality
Multiple distribution channels		Innovative digital platform
Digital capability and open banking		Digital money-management tools
Multi-product customers		Limited back-end legacy systems

FIGURE 8

Virgin Money's strategic position

Before the CYBG acquisition, Virgin Money's main service channels were digital: 79 percent of sales took place digitally. In credit cards the figure was 99 percent! On the CYBG side, digital adoption was only at 48 percent in 2019.[37] At the end of 2020, the combined personal digital adoption was at 56 percent (up 5 percent from 2019).

While Virgin Money's primary sales channel is digital, face-to-face service is also strategically important. Many banks are reducing personal services and optimizing time spent at branches, but Virgin Money sees personal encounters as an important part of strengthening the customer relationship; and it sees branches—or stores—as a "new generation of creative and community-focused spaces giving everybody a space to learn, work and play."

In addition to its "stores," Virgin Money has exclusive customer lounges, the sole purpose of which is to create great customer experiences. The idea behind the lounges is to enable customers to relax and feel that they are part of a community. The lounges are not there to offer banking services but to be a touchpoint to the company's brand, to embody Virgin Money's service culture to build long-lasting and deep customer relationships. Every lounge is different; you can bowl in one while another has a movie theatre and a working and relaxation space resembling a plane.

Virgin Money has been a trailblazer with its lounge concept. Several years after opening the first Virgin Money lounge, many recent articles and reports note that, in the future, bank branches will become service lounges or experience centers that feature casual seating areas, advice and deeper conversations with representatives and the community.[38]

Customers at the Heart of Everything

The foundation of the customer experience at an airport is a basic process: the ability for customers to pass through the checkpoints efficiently and make it to their flights on time. In banking, the "basic process" consists of the customer's feeling that her finances are in order, that the bank's products are good and that customer service is simple and transparent. Simply put, customers are asking for time and flexibility. Basis processes form the foundation for building not only a strong customer relationship, but also a larger share of all of the customer's banking needs.

Virgin Money seeks to create a continuously positive experience for all its customers regardless of the length of the relationship, channel or banking need. Building on the Virgin companies' best practices, Virgin Money is building its customer experience on three main pillars: digital-first, spatial (feel-good physical experiences) and human (conversations, not transactions), and has the target to be named as one of the UK's top three institutions in banking service quality by 2022.

Many of the accolades Virgin Money has received are related to its way of listening to customers and responding to feedback. Part of the credit goes to a Virgin Money program that listens to and interprets customer feedback in real time, handles complaints and improves experiences (Virgin Money made it to the UK Complaint Handling Awards Hall of Fame in 2020). And part of the credit goes to the company's measurement of customer happiness through an innovative "Smile" score.

Transformation Journey

Before being acquired by CYBG, Virgin Money was building a digital bank of the next generation. It had committed 38 million British pounds ($54 million USD) to build a completely new digital banking system that would be based on the efficient use of data and the customer experience—and offering personalized accounts.

The new digital bank was planned to be launched in 2019, but before it was brought to market, Virgin Money decided to cancel the project and migrate all of its brands to CYBG's existing digital platform (iB). The iB platform is built, integrated and scaled using a private cloud, open architecture and robotics. A big data platform supports a single customer view, and decisioning systems facilitate better understanding of the customers. The digital platform enables all the services you would expect from a traditional bank plus many of the features and ways of working you typically get from start-ups.

iB was designed for the world of open banking. One of its core strengths is an open API capability that has allowed Virgin Money to partner with a variety of fintech and other players like Virgin service partners. Whether streamlining the search and application process for mortgages or using existing direct debits to compare prices on gas, electricity and fuel, the partnerships create unique offerings matching customer lifestyles and expanding customer propositions.[39]

Merging two companies is never easy and straightforward. Establishing Virgin Money as the sole brand, migrating all the users onto a single platform and unifying digital operations has been a huge undertaking. Yet CYBG and Virgin Money have created a serious full-service national competitor to the status quo in UK banking with clear focus and ambition to excel in customer service and experience. Virgin Money has grown from an innovative fintech firm to a digital-first bank with 6.4 million customers.

And the investments and efforts are starting to pay off. In May 2021, Virgin Money announced a strong first half of the year, returning to profit for the first time since 2019. With a trusted and recognized brand and digital capability with a single open banking digital platform to support all of its customers, Virgin Money is well positioned to serve customers with a world-class experience and deliver on its purpose of "Making you happier about money."

A brand, a customer experience based on the brand and the ability to collect data and create customer-centric products and services that make people's lives better are the competitive advantages of banking in the future. Analytics, open API and cloud services will continue to grow across the sector. Innovations and the ability to operate them on a large scale safely will separate the wheat from the chaff. Regulation will shake the borders of banking, customer expectations will change and grow and, simultaneously, new digital banks and players will invest first and foremost in customer experience with the belief that a customer interface victory will improve relationships, loyalty and profits.

The pandemic has shown that not only are customers looking to engage with digital channels, but more and more they are looking for support to meet their financial goals. The increased number of interactions and the ability to track and understand these interactions gives retail banks further insights into the customers that in turn can help refine and improve the experience. There are many examples of best-in-class work related to the customer's digital experience: NatWest in the UK is focused on personalization, BBVA has an award-winning mobile app (and you do not even have to be a customer to use it!) and Caixabank has managed to bring together customer data across the web, mobile and ATMs. But it remains to be seen who can first connect all the parts.

In the wildest visions, the provider of the banking customer experience is separate from the actual institution holding the deposits and balances. It remains to be seen what role the traditional banks will assume in the future and who consumers will bank with.

HOSPITALITY AND TRAVEL: HOTELS

Travel and hospitality has experienced a huge shift over the past few years, first due to digitalization and now to the global pandemic. The customer experience in the hospitality industry consists of improvements provided by new technology and innovation and traditional well-proven principles.

The hospitality industry remains labor intensive. Personal service provided by people plays a significant role in building a good customer experience. However, it has become impossible to compete only by providing excellent service. Customers expect excellent service and a good, justified price as a starting point. But they want much more than that. They also want easy access and good usability during the whole customer experience process.

Besides service, there are other ways to influence and compete for customers' attention. Customers want businesses to meet their personal needs, be socially responsible and offer long-term partnership rather than one-off engagements. Loyalty has gone way beyond the plastic loyalty card we used to carry in our wallet. We want to be part of a community of like-minded people. A true loyal customer relationship is based on identifying a shared lifestyle, values and interests. Success in hospitality starts with understanding the customer's hopes, dreams and needs.

Staying Home

While many businesses have been struggling due to the Covid-19 pandemic, the hospitality and travel industry was among the hardest hit. Hospitality and tourism businesses have been struggling to recoup the losses they sustained because of the pandemic. According to the World Travel & Tourism Council, the first ten months of 2020 alone resulted in $935 billion of lost revenue for the global tourism industry.[40] And in the US alone, hotels are expected to lose $112 billion due to coronavirus. The total loss in economic output will be nine times the impact of 9/11 on US travel revenues.[41]

The year 2020 was one of the worst on record for hotels and unfortunately 2021 did not look much better. Travel restrictions, stay-at-home orders, mandatory tests and quarantines and, most important, travelers' ongoing fears of getting infected stopped leisure travel almost completely. Business travel experienced an even bigger hit.

Some innovative hospitality players have managed to restart and rebuild their businesses by pivoting to new business models or strategies such as providing staycations for locals and delivering room service to people's homes (during lockdown we absolutely loved the Berkeley hotel breakfast in bed at home!).[42] Many hotels in the big cities have also begun to cooperate with delivery companies like Uber Eats. The use of digital technologies has accelerated and businesses that were the most prepared to adapt new (digital) services have survived the best, as they have as in every industry.

The future will show whether we return to pre-pandemic levels of airline and hotel bookings. In a July 2020 survey of hospitality executives, 65 percent said they believed that bookings would recover after nine-plus months yet, as of this writing on the verge of the 2021 summer holiday season, travel agencies report summer holiday demand shifting to autumn due to uncertainties.

After months (almost years!) of sitting at home, we all miss the adventures leisure travel was able to offer and we do foresee people traveling as soon as it is allowed again.[43] For example, the day after the announcement of "green list" countries, the UK recorded a boom in holiday sales for travel companies.[44]

The recovery of business travel is a bigger question mark. It seems unlikely that we will return to normal and more likely that business travel will experience the same drastic change that we are seeing with the return to offices. It may become rare to have a dedicated seat at the office going forward as more and more companies like Twitter, Salesforce and Spotify are embracing fully the freedom of their employees to work from home as long as they like.

Toward the New Normal

Hospitality and travel businesses are increasingly expected to possess digital readiness and ability. Digitalization increases and intensifies competition as the enhanced transparency makes it easier for consumers to compare experiences and algorithms help us locate the best offers. This leads to a pressure to increase efficiency to maintain growth and profitability in the industry.

Already years ago, consumers moved to digital channels when searching for information on holidays, hotels and travel options, booking tickets and accommodation and sharing reviews and pictures at different forums. Almost all communication that happens before and after travel is handled digitally.

Platforms Offer Consumers Alternatives and Bargaining Power

The travel sector has historically been slow to react to the changes brought on by digitalization. A decade ago, new travel booking services were developed by new entrants, not the traditional travel agencies. (Do you remember when we picked up travel brochures from kiosks and booked tickets at brick-and-mortar offices?) The same phenomenon happened with online booking for hotels. Expedia, Booking.com and other digital platforms brought their services to market faster than hotel chains. Only with competitive pressure brought on by these services did the hotel chains start working on their platforms. Now they are forced to try to lure consumers back to the hotels' websites. Hotels seek to improve their margins by trying to get consumers to book directly by offering better pricing and special offers such as breakfast included.

Booking.com recently made an interesting change in its mission statement. Previously it concentrated on optimizing the booking process and offering an easy and smooth booking service for every budget and every accommodation. This is no longer enough as customers expect real value-add in return for their loyalty. In its new mission statement, Booking.com promises to "make it easy for everyone to discover the world." Time will show how they will manage to operationalize this promise. Booking.com has been one of the digital success stories in the travel sector. Over its twenty-year history, it has become one of the largest travel portals globally and its vision has always been extremely customer-centric.

The World Economic Forum predicts that there will be a significant change in how revenues are split between traditional players and new challengers. Online Travel Agencies (OTAs) will continue to increase their market share in the coming years and grab a growing piece of the accommodation-booking revenues. Accommodation providers are predicted to lose an increasing share of their revenues to digital booking services such as Expedia and Booking.com, which attract an ever-increasing number of consumers by offering highly advanced digital services. In central booking services, price plays an important role in the purchasing decision; hence they weaken hotels' margins and opportunities to differentiate themselves.

Hotels are also struggling with their profitability due to the shift to alternative accommodation options such as Airbnb. With over seven million listings worldwide (2021), Airbnb is well positioned to maintain and grow its market share. Even in the middle of the pandemic (2021), it is still attracting fourteen thousand new hosts to the platform each month. As of May 2021, Airbnb was valued at $91 billion.

The laws of the platform economy also apply in the accommodation business: the biggest platforms win the most customers. The booking platforms present accommodation options suited to consumers based on algorithms; they rely on customer reviews to do the rest. Consumers trust TripAdvisor reviews almost as much as recommendations from friends. They choose accommodations based on ratings and ignore providers who don't respond to questions and comments online.

It's not only the newcomers that are changing the industry, however. The traditional hotel chains have long tried to figure out the future of traveling. Marriott International is the largest hotel chain in the world. It leaves even the second largest player, Hilton, far behind. Marriott operates in more than 125 countries and manages 6,500+ properties.

Marriott is investing heavily in digitalization and it leans on new technologies in its growth strategy. A couple of years ago, Marriott opened an innovation lab (Upscale Charlotte, NC Hotel | Charlotte Marriott City Center), where it seeks to develop new concepts for the hotel of the future.[45] With this experiment, Marriott is a front-runner among the traditional hotel chains in leveraging technology to both improve the customer experience and to make their operations more efficient.

A few years ago, Marriott began collaborating with Amazon and brought Alexa into select Marriott hotels. The customers in these hotels can use voice control to order a bottle of bubbly from room service, choose their preferred pillows from the pillow menu, or control the room temperature, lighting and air-conditioning. Alexa will also play music and give tips on local sights.

By 2014, Marriott was offering its customers the opportunity to try virtual traveling in phone booth–looking devices that took the customers to a future Marriott hotel and onward to admire the views at the beaches of Hawaii with the help of 4D sensor technology and a virtual reality headset. The slight breeze in the hair, light spray of water on the face and rays of the sun generated a new "travel experience." While traveling will probably never become fully virtual, the technology may usher in new kinds of experiences in new countries and cultures. This booth would have been handy during the pandemic. Many of us would love to have traveled somewhere, even virtually, after orchestrating the home-schooling chaos!

Hotel chains have also begun to understand the power of customer data. They have endless sources to gather information about their customers: online and on-site behavior, social media channels, loyalty programs, even search history and previous engagements and conversations with the chain. Data will allow hotels to provide more personalized experiences during the stay, along with the ability to constantly communicate and engage with the customers through different channels. This is transforming the one-off stays into ongoing engagements and relationships.

Robots Are Coming

The travel industry has been significant to the global economy. Hospitality accounted for 10 percent of global GDP and was growing steadily since the economic downturn in 2008–2009 until the pandemic. Now we are seeing serious warning signs of a severe drop that may take years to recover from. The World Travel & Tourism Council calculates that the Covid-19 pandemic could lead to a loss of fifty million jobs in the hospitality industry worldwide.[46]

Temporary workers were the first to be hit, but the pandemic's impact has also been felt by permanent employees as the hospitality industry continues to be hard-pressed to cut costs due to a lack of customers. The pandemic has also caused a lot of fear and personal struggles that have forced people to move closer to their families and friends. Many frontline workers in hotels and restaurants have moved to other industries to secure a monthly paycheck. And many of them will not return if the pandemic continues.

This mass employee escape could have a severe impact on the talent available in the industry and may cause problems when the industry starts to grow again. As of this writing, on the eve of the UK lifting all restrictions, the country is reporting a shortfall of 188,000 hospitality workers and many hospitality owners from New York to Florida are struggling to open their venues at full capacity due to a shortage of employees.[47]

Going forward, hotels and restaurants will move to leaner and more efficient operations, where a balance between smart digital tools and skilled labor is optimized. This will serve both the needs of the hoteliers and the customers. Hotels are using new technologies like AI and robotics to improve productivity and efficiency. But it's not only the cost savings that are driving digitalization in the hospitality industry. Customers want extended service hours, they want information that is always available at the click of a button and they want 24/7 services during their stay, along with loyalty programs for when they return.

We have seen the first robot-staffed hotel in Japan. Henn-na Hotel in Nagasaki is entirely staffed by robots.[48] At the front desk you will engage with a robot, who will handle the check-in and check-out procedures (in case you haven't done those online yourself). Storage is run by another robot and there are many of them providing information regarding services and different activities. Voice and facial recognition technologies help them serve you in an effective and accurate manner. Based on customer ratings (3.8), the robots still have some work to do to satisfy the customers, but the trend toward automation and robotics is here to stay.

In housekeeping, hotels are implementing high-tech solutions to keep guestrooms not only clean, but nowadays also sterilized. Automated vacuums working with the demanding tasks autonomously (they can easily clean the dust under the heavy furniture) allow the housekeeping to focus on organizing things and doing the last mile. Robots help hold the labor costs in control by decreasing the time to clean rooms. Bots are here to make our stay at the hotels safer using UV light and sprays to kill viruses.

In the future, hotels will be able to offer personalized butler service provided by a robot. M Hotel Singapore has used robotics for years. It employs the robot-butler AURA. The reaction from customers has been positive and even surprising. It has been easier to ask for services from a robot than from a human as many people are embarrassed to ask for services from another human; for example, it may be more comfortable to ask a robot for a new toothbrush when you have forgotten to bring yours from home. AURA has helped the hotel staff to save on average five hours a day. This time has been used for training the staff to ensure personalized service.

There are many other use cases for robots in hotels and airports. The next few years will show how much we are able to reduce the price of operations and maintenance to make robots an attractive alternative to human labor.

Travel Habits Are Changing

The continuing crisis has had a profound impact on travel habits, preferences, players and the entire industry. In 2021, at the time of writing this book, traveling is less about tourism and short visits to different countries and more about living and working away from home. Remote working and remote schooling have offered flexibility for people to change their location after many months of staying at home. According to an Airbnb survey in 2020, there has been a 128 percent increase in willingness to relocate to a new country, city or neighborhood.[49] The traditional lines between vacations and working have been blurred, giving Airbnb and other holiday rental companies an opportunity to compete with accommodation options suitable for people who need more space for longer stays and who want to combine everyday life with days off.

Outside the long-term stays, most travel in 2020 and 2021 happened close to home and staycations have become the biggest traveling trend. According to Global Web Index, globally almost half of all holiday travelers are planning a domestic vacation and more than 30 percent a local staycation.[50] Despite missing the overseas experience, the sustainability and environmental benefits of near-distance travel and supporting local entrepreneurs are predicted to influence our travel behaviors after Covid-19. We are also seeing the advanced AR technologies taking us around the world without moving away from our own couches. This is what Marriott tried with its traveling booth pilot.

Consumers continue to leverage digital services extensively and, in the future, they will book their trips directly from their own couches using voice recognition. Different kinds of voice-guided services will become mainstream and the alternatives available to customers will be filtered more efficiently with the help of algorithms and user data. It will be interesting to see if history repeats itself. Will the hotels' digital development projects progress slowly (like with digital booking systems decade ago), leaving an opportunity for third parties to occupy the vacant space?

Digital-first and digital-only companies are typically more agile to innovate new solutions. (See figure 9 on establishing new business models.) The hospitality and travel industries will have to look for partners or recruit new expertise to ensure staying current, not to mention to lead with their digital offering. Half of the travel, hospitality and dining brands are already leveraging partners to accelerate their digital transformation. The days of transactional digital services are over. Customers want value-added services and engagement.

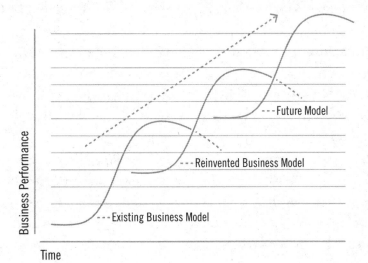

FIGURE 9

*Establishing a new business model takes time; change should be initiated
ahead of time even if the current cash flow remains strong.*

Tailored to You

It is already possible to book a seat on a plane before the
flight. In the future it will also be possible to book a specific
room at a hotel. A check-in service is often available on mobile; however, that is rarely the case with choosing a room.
Particularly in hotels where every room is different, many customers would like to have a say in choosing their room themselves. Currently the available options are limited to floor and
proximity to an elevator.

Even the controls in the room are going mobile: adjusting
the air-conditioning and many other services will be conducted with a tablet or a mobile device. Technology will play
a bigger role in these smart rooms. In the past, television was

the height of hotel room technology. Many hotels still offer entertainment packages consisting of decades-old movies and an adult-entertainment channel behind a PIN code. This in a time when 90 percent of customers carry a device that gives them access to various entertainment options such as Spotify and Netflix. Hence, free and excellent Wi-Fi is a necessity.

Hotels are also updating the room interiors by replacing the seldom-used closets (most travelers never take their stuff out of their bags) with functional space solutions such as bringing sports equipment to the millennials' rooms; wellbeing is one of today's biggest trends. In the US, fitness chain Equinox has already opened its first hotels that focus on sports and wellbeing.

Many hotel chains also have their own brands for different customer segments. Moxy by Marriott and Tru by Hilton offer smaller rooms but have a greater focus on communal spaces. Millennials want to engage with others and build networks. The room is for sleeping. These hotels offer great facilities to work. The customers are now also scanning the hotel facilities around the hotel buildings. Outdoor travel is the biggest trend and has been predicted to recover the fastest. After the pandemic, we will see even more serious efforts from hotel chains to tap into changing traveler demand.[51]

Good Service Will Be Remembered Longer Than a Good Price

In the hospitality business, the most important variable from the customer experience point of view remains service: the role of personal and physical encounters. Before the pandemic, for example, the fastest growing hotel segment in the

US was boutique hotels that offered personalized, unique, service-oriented experiences. On the other hand, at a time when business models are changing due to digitalization, focusing only on service has caused headaches for many hospitality entrepreneurs.

Different customers have different needs. Some will forgive small deficiencies in the process in return for good service, but the digitally native generation prioritizes a smooth digital customer experience, even at the expense of traditional service. Therefore, developing the business is a constant balancing act between services and self-services. How does a hotel manifest the physical experience in the virtual world? How does it align the processes, the governance and the business models in the best and most efficient way? One should carefully evaluate which parts impacting the customer experience can be digitalized, automated or removed; and which parts of excellent service provided by another person will generate the best customer experience.

First and foremost, good service should be personalized based on a strong understanding of the customer. New technologies combining data on online behavior with the customer profile will enable the foundation for a scalable personalization. The gap between the forerunners and the traditional operators will continue to grow. In the US, 89 percent of hospitality businesses that personalized their services reported that the experiment resulted in increased revenue.[52]

Frustratingly often, the service experience doesn't change regardless of which customer profile options you choose. Also, hotel websites will often suggest the same additional services to everybody, even if your search criteria or the additional information in the booking you have made already indicates that you are a family rather than a couple. Previously, customers were happy with a good quality standardized customer experience. Now hotels are expected to profile customers to certain target groups based on values and expectations.

HOTELIER ERIC TOREN'S MASTERPIECE HOTEL, TWENTYSEVEN, MAKES YOUR DREAMS COME TRUE

There are many hotels in Amsterdam but only one that is led with a passion like no other. A little boutique hotel, TwentySeven, standing majestically next to the famous Dam Square, is hotelier Eric Toren's longtime dream come true. Eric has extensive experience in the hospitality industry from many award-winning hotel chains. After traveling around the world and working in many countries, he returned to his home country and began a list of ideas for the hotel of his dreams. A few years later, TwentySeven opened its doors to its first customers. The concept is unique. It's a dream hotel without traditional five-star services such as a spa or a pool. It doesn't even have a gym, but instead offers something so special that loyal guests return again and again.

"You can't focus on things you don't have. We have so many other things to offer and we focus on them. We make things private. Everyone has their own steam room and a jacuzzi in their room. We also bring workout equipment whenever needed," says Eric when asked how he can compete in a world of hotel booking portals where people search options based on services and easily compare price vs. quality. "We have the best restaurant, bar and suites and what really makes us unique is our knowledge of making experiences. This is beyond the traditional service, even if exceptional."

And indeed, the hotel really feels like an experience from the first moment when you enter the old, charismatic building and see the smiling face of the piccolo offering you a glass of champagne. Every customer has a butler, and the room feels way better than in pictures. "You have to exceed the customer expectations from the first moment. We don't have stylists to prepare the rooms for the online pictures, and the customer always gets more than they expected. We don't want to put all the cards on the table right away," Eric explains. There are too many examples of the opposite in this industry.

What makes this dream hotel so special then? "People want to belong. You need to create a place where your customers really want to be part of it. They want more than just a bed. They want to follow others; celebrities, thought leaders, similar thinkers. They want to get entertained and make memories to cherish. We treat everybody in the same way, from the Royal family to any guest visiting." Based on surveys, this is true. Customers want to buy products and services that represent their values; they want the opportunity to be surrounded with others who see the world through the same lens.

Every hotel aims to provide good service. Some seem to succeed better. What separates the best? "The hospitality industry will have a big challenge after the Covid-19 pandemic is over," Eric explains. "Many of the employees have already moved to other industries and they will not come back easily. We will see an enormous lack of talent. We take good care of our people and make them stay!"

In the TwentySeven Hotel, memorable experiences are created with a combination of people and technology. "In my hotel, 50 percent of the experience comes from the character of the employees and 50 percent are the back-end systems." Eric has created his own management software solution that gives him the visibility he needs. Technology ensures the employees have the data they need to be able to focus on the customers. Every detail is double- or triple-checked. For example, in case the lead person doesn't confirm the right number of clean wineglasses for a dinner, the manager will get a notification. If no one reacts in time, the information goes all the way up to Eric himself. There is no room for mistakes.

"Technology is hugely important in today's hospitality. It's everywhere," says Eric. "You need to have systems that work from the booking to the check-in, during your stay and long after you have left the hotel." Technology plays a critical role at TwentySeven. How is the other 50 percent managed then? Customers ask for more and more, and if things are not working, you can read all about it online the next day. Every customer has the power to influence.

"The customer is always right," Eric says. "Your reality is your customer's reality. We see things in a different way, and even if there is an explanation, your customer doesn't want to hear it. They want to get the issues corrected." And you need to get things right as soon as possible. It's too late to return to your customers when they have left the building already. They want to have the best experience while visiting.

According to Eric, "There are no differences between the different cultures or nationalities when it comes to service. The difference is that in some countries you can hire double personnel for the same money. But this doesn't guarantee that your service is any better." Indeed, many of us have had experiences in countries where "no" is not an accepted response to a customer. You always get "yes" as a response and then nothing gets done.

When asked about the secret formula of his passion and success, Eric smiles and finally says, "I'm probably the only therapist as a hotelier in the world. I think I understand better and better what people like and need." This is easy to agree with when listening to his stories.

When walking away from the hotel with a big smile on my face and a funny, mysterious bubbly feeling inside of me, I'm still wondering how he makes it happen. This is the last mile beyond all the little details. It's the sixth sense the best hoteliers have.

CASE: Hotel Zoku Amsterdam

Hotel Zoku Amsterdam, opened in 2016, is a hotel concept praised in many business magazines and by its customers. It concentrates mainly on the needs of young business travelers. It is interesting that the hospitality industry's own publications have noted Zoku in their ratings, even though it doesn't represent a traditional four-star hotel with modernized services. However, Zoku has received top ratings from customers in almost every booking portal.

The concept behind Zoku is the result of extensive crowdsourcing and research efforts the team did before opening. Zoku's accommodation units or "lofts" consist of a (bunk) bed in addition to a small kitchen and a working space. Zoku leans on the idea of the "death" of traditional hotel rooms. Its concept combines the best parts of Airbnb from home-like accommodations and convenience to communal working.

The loft could easily be a young person's first city apartment. Zoku does actually hope that some of its customers need a place to stay for a longer period.

It is true that an increasing number of people work without a regard for time and place and many tasks are project-like, so longer-term accommodation in different cities is needed. Renting, with its long agreement processes, is rigid; and Airbnb doesn't fit with the limited and centralized travel policies of many businesses. Invariably, business trips are booked via centralized corporate portals where Airbnb is not an option. With its communal working spaces, Zoku also offers something that Airbnb is not able to offer.[53]

Zoku has won the Radical Innovation Award, which is given to new kinds of hotel concepts. The jury justified the win by highlighting Zoku's ability to take into account the change in people's needs and behavior brought on by digitalization as work is transforming from a nine-to-five job to a lifestyle. Work should be provided the right kind of facilities, regardless of time and place.

"The advance of technology has changed personal and professional lifestyles," says Hans Meyer, Zoku's cofounder and managing director.[54] "Boundaries between work and leisure are fading and blurring borders have made people more mobile than ever."

Zoku in Amsterdam is the first, but despite the pandemic, new Zoku Hotels were opened in the spring of 2021 in Copenhagen and Vienna. Zoku in Paris was set to open in 2022.

Services for the New Generations

What makes Zoku different? In the hotel, almost all customary processes and services have been reimagined. This makes the experience almost confusing at first. There is no real reception desk, but the customer arrives in a social space that combines all the functions from a restaurant and a bar in an office-like working space. The customer checks in herself at a computer that has been provided for the purpose. If the activation fails, she can request help from a "sidekick" (there are no reception professionals or waiters in the hotel) who bustles around the social space supporting customers.

The Zoku app provides all the information customers need about the hotel's programs and services. Checking out is done with a mobile device, as is purchasing additional services.

The Zoku restaurant operates in the same fashion. A customer places an order on a computer and prints a receipt. Once finished with her meal, she takes the dishes to the dish trolley herself. The atmosphere is really more like an office than a hotel; this image is further enhanced by the availability of various board games and Ping-Pong. The experience is based on self-service, but it is very social. Instead of small restaurant tables, there are communal tables that make it easy to meet new people. Obviously the Wi-Fi is outstanding and works everywhere in the building.

The hotel has shaped its services to be congenial with millennials. Housekeeping is provided every second day. It is available every day if requested, but is not recommended for environmental reasons. This is compatible with the values of many visitors. The hotel overall is environmentally friendly.

All its operations from heating to lighting have been designed with environmental considerations in mind. The are no minibars, but there is a fridge in every room. Plastic water bottles are not recommended. Instead of room service, there is a 24/7 "Everything Store" in the social space. There is no gym in the hotel, but they cooperate with a CrossFit space next door, which is now also more popular than a traditional gym.

Zoku offers everything the new millennial customer group expects from accommodation services. It will also meet the post-pandemic travel needs well.

HOSPITALITY AND TRAVEL: AIRPORTS

Airports and runways have existed for more than a century. The Hamburg Airport, which opened in 1911, is among the oldest airports still in use. As the aviation business opened up, the number of air passengers grew increasingly along with it and more airports were built. They also grew in size. Discount carriers made air travel accessible to the masses and changed the competition between airports.

And then Covid-19 hit. Airplanes were grounded, and in cities where one was used to seeing an airplane fly over every fifteen seconds, the sky was suddenly empty. As were the airports. Of all the businesses affected by the pandemic, the aviation industry, along with the hospitality and travel sector, is definitely one of the hardest hit. The year 2020 marked the end of a decade of consistent growth in global passenger traffic. According to Airports Council International, international passenger volume in 2020 ended below one billion passengers—a decrease of 75 percent compared to 2019![55]

Airport revenues are directly correlated with air traffic. While the portfolio of non-aeronautical activities may have made the situation easier for some airports, most were forced to close parts of the terminal, put planned expansion or improvement projects on hold, furlough or fire staff and try to find ways to leverage their facilities and equipment for alternative projects or community support to protect their business.

Covid-19 has also impacted airport operations: focus on retail experiences and value-added services has completely shifted to cleanliness, health, self-service and automation. Global vaccination efforts offer hope to restarting travel and the airports are working with all the stakeholders to ensure a return to normal. It remains to be seen what the new normal means for the airport customer experience and if the customer expectations for the airport experience have changed. For example, will consumers accept anything as long as they are free to fly, or has Covid-19 increased our expectations for airport operations? And are the changes we are now experiencing here to stay?

Airport operations were extensively regulated already before the added health safety requirements. In this kind of environment, how do we discuss designing experiences?

Continuum of Experiences

Before the pandemic, the airport experience included sweating in the queue to the security check, stuffing liquids into small plastic bags, noise and crowds. The customer had to provide the same details about herself at multiple points, the processes were repetitive, communication imperfect and the experience not personalized.

As a result of Covid-19, airports look and feel pretty different: first of all, they are mostly empty. But additionally, as of this writing, social-distancing measures have been put in place with warning signs visible throughout the airport building. Everything that can be converted to self-service has been; and processes have become touchless, minimizing the contact between staff and the passengers. Lounges, most restaurants, shops and other facilities are closed.

For those who considered the airport as a compulsory stop at the beginning and end of each journey, the current experience is an improvement. Indeed, the latest annual edition of the ACI Airport Service Quality Barometer concludes that overall passenger satisfaction has increased since the start of the pandemic.[56] This is likely a result of the change in passenger demographics, but also the faster processes due to the low number of fellow passengers. Suddenly it is possible to find a parking spot in the lot closest to the terminal. And with no queues, passing through the airport is a breeze.

Pandemic or not, the airport is not often at the top of the list of positive customer experience environments. Yet, experience matters. Already a third of passengers choose their flight route based on the reputation of the airports and the customer experiences attached to them, especially when considering connecting flights.[57] At Singapore's Changi Airport, one can visit a park that spans over five floors, admire the world's largest indoor waterfall and explore labyrinths. Munich Airport is great with kids (they can play outdoors), and you can relax in a library at Schiphol Airport in Amsterdam. Also, passengers who can choose their departure and return airports make their decisions based on the passenger experience and the airport reputation: two-thirds of Europeans live within a two-hour drive from at least two airports.

To a passenger, the airport customer experience feels like a single experience. In reality, it is a chain, or a continuum, of experiences provided by several separate vendors that the passengers do not necessarily know about. When you are talking about having to wait for your bags for an eternity in London, do you say, "Very slow service at London Heathrow" or "Very slow service by cargo company X"? The next time you are planning for a trip, you are probably only thinking of the slow service at Heathrow, not finding out if the same company handles the cargo at all the other airports as well.

In a normal airport experience during which the passenger parks her car, checks in, drops her bags, goes through security check, shows her passport, buys a book, drinks a coffee, visits a restroom and boards a plane, she uses the services of, on average, ten different vendors. When using the services of well-known brands such as Starbucks or Burger King, she is conscious of the vendor, but with many services offered their provider is not known to the customer.

Of those ten services, there might be only one or two that are provided by the airport operator: the customer may have parked her car at a parking lot operated by the airport operator and checked her flight details on an information screen. The rest of the services are provided by customs and immigration officers, security firms, cafeterias, restaurants, shops and spas. How is it possible to offer a pleasant customer experience in such a fragmented environment? Can the airport operator take responsibility for the customer experience at the airport? What is the airport operator's role in it?

Despite the fragmented nature of the airport ecosystem, the airport operator is the only player with a direct relationship to all of the relevant parties, commercial operators, airlines and passengers. Their role in the air traffic value chain is central.

The airport operator defines the customer experience strategy for the airport—what the experience at this particular airport should feel like and how to measure success. The airport operator creates and gives guidelines on a holistic customer experience to the other players, providing customer experience training and encouraging cooperation among operators. Ultimately the quality is ensured with service-level agreements. Naturally, global brands have their own approaches regarding the customer experience. The intriguing challenge is to bring all of these together and offer a harmonious experience.

A Good Customer Experience at an Airport

The customer experience at an airport is always defined by time. The first priority (and concern) of the passenger is to make it to the plane on time. A smooth basic process is the cornerstone of the experience. If it is not working, all the other elements designed to augment it will not be able to compensate for it. The customers must feel that they are in control, that they can move around the airport without delays, disruption or confusion.

The traditional methods of improving the experience at the airport have been adding clear signs, providing more seating in places where the passengers wait and guiding passengers with announcements. The number of announcements were increased, until given up almost completely due to the noise they bring. For example, when the Helsinki-Vantaa Airport in Finland gave up announcements in 2015, there were more than a thousand of them a day! The Silent Airport concept is in use at many key airports and is a growing airport wellness trend.

Minimizing the message overload to the senses is the key factor in improving the airport customer experience. Today, improved flight information display systems guide the passengers and self-service kiosks and mobile apps help with scheduling the visit, keeping track of flight time and moving around the airport. Through the apps, you can queue virtually or make (pre)orders to restaurants and cafes, avoiding the queues and holdups. There are also mobile and online services geared toward supporting travel in pandemic and post-pandemic times. Changi Airport in Singapore recently launched a new Safe Travel Concierge, an online service that helps passengers book their on-arrival Covid-19 tests and check that they have all the necessary pre-travel documentation in place.

Having enough restrooms and making sure that they are clean is also part of a smooth basic process. In airport customer satisfaction surveys, the passengers invariably say that clean sanitation facilities are one of the most important factors in measuring the success of the airport customer experience. According to a study conducted at Orlando International Airport, the customers were neither too bothered about the queues at the security checks nor particularly interested in shopping opportunities.[58] The majority were just hoping to make it to their flight on time and to use a clean restroom before they boarded. As a result of the pandemic, cleanliness and a hygienic experience are more important than before.

Beyond the basics and the smooth process, some passengers appreciate modern facilities, playful experiences and innovative solutions. Some appreciate when the experience offers a local flavor. Instead of a faceless and international experience, people look for the special characteristics, brands and experiences particular to the country where the airport is located. At the Incheon International Airport in Seoul, passengers can visit a museum of Korean culture. At the Rovaniemi Airport in Finland, passengers can enjoy the décor, appreciate the arctic nature and try the reindeer meatballs and reindeer soup in the cafeteria.

The Importance of Customer Experience to the Airport Business

Airlines and commercial operators such as restaurants and shops are the business-to-business customers of airports. As an example, Finavia, the Finnish operator of airports, gets two-thirds of its revenue from airlines and a third from commercial operators. The revenues from commercial operators vary significantly between airports based on passenger numbers and service offerings. At Seoul's Incheon Airport, the profits from tax-free sales alone are larger than the entire annual running costs of the Hartsfield-Jackson Atlanta International Airport.

However, the end customers of all airport services and hence of the airports themselves are the passengers. Even though some airports, particularly the number two airports of big cities, have begun to compete on price and offer access to low-cost carries at affordable rates, most of the airports want to (and must) attract customers by providing positive experiences. Every passenger brings revenue at least equal to the airport fee (via the ticket) and possibly also by the services they use, such as separate parking fees.

The costs of operating an airport are always high, especially fixed costs. Running it is strictly regulated. To increase their profits, many airports have sought to renew their operating models and earnings logic by concentrating on non-aeronautical revenues. Research has confirmed a positive correlation between a good airport customer experience and the amount of money spent at the airport. Airports Council International (ACI) estimates that a 1 percent increase in customer satisfaction increases non-aeronautical-related profits by 1.5 percent.

Some international airport operators have long known that when customer-passengers have more time and less stress, they are more likely to spend money in the shops and on the services. Happy customers spend on average 10 percent more at airports than unsatisfied ones and up to 20 percent more on tax-free goods.

Digitalization and Airports

At best, digitalization can be a game changer for all airport functions. On the one hand it may enhance capacity usage and cut costs; on the other hand it may increase profits. The Internet of Things, smart buildings and digital service points enable the optimization of space and processes. Sensors, cameras and Bluetooth technology enable the optimal flow of passengers. iBeacons provide contextual notifications and relevant offers.

In the near future most of the basic service encounters will be handled with devices, biometric scanning or robots. The introduction of touchless technologies has accelerated due to the pandemic resulting in more (touchless) self-service check-ins, self-scanning of boarding passes and automated border control using biometrics. For years at Terminal 4 in Singapore's Changi Airport, facial recognition technology has been shortening the length of manual inspections. The passengers are able to check in, drop their bags, pass customs control and board the plane by self-service with the aid of a biometric system. Now Singapore is targeting iris and facial biometrics as part of its New Clearance Concept at all checkpoints.[59]

The Smart Tunnel at the Dubai International Airport removes the need for a security check. When a passenger passes through the tunnel, AI with facial recognition handles the process and passengers are cleared through immigration without human intervention. It will not be long before "hands in your pockets" travel will be completely ordinary. There will no longer be a need for travel documents.

Increasing commercial activity with multichannel retail sales solutions and increasing the time that passengers have for spending will give the airports an opportunity to grow business and stand out. Navigating the airport will become easier with the help of technology, and the commercial operators will be able to make personalized offers based on each customer's personal preferences, previous purchase history, frequent flyer program or interests in social media. For example, Heathrow Airport has taken an approach to promoting products and services before, during and after travel through personalized messages. And what an impact it has on revenues! The airport reports 60 percent higher average spending among customers who receive targeted and relevant offers.[60]

And it is no longer even required to visit the shops at the airport. Many airports offer "reserve and collect" shopping where passengers can purchase products online from many different vendors and terminals before they arrive at the airport, and even during their trip. The delivery point can even be your departure gate!

With digitalization, customers expect the airport services and experience to have the same level of personalization, context-relevance and ease as banking and retail shopping experiences. When in a bank, a customer can only see the information in her own bank account. So when she is in an airport, why should she have to search through hundreds of departing flights for the details of hers? Soon she will not have to. Delta Air Lines announced in January 2020 that its PARALLEL REALITY™ technology, which leverages multi-view pixels, will allow multiple customers to see personalized content tailored to them on a single screen, at the same time and in their preferred language.[61]

> We're not chasing shiny objects or tech for the sake of being cool. We are dedicated to solving your travel problems and making your voyages—and your lives—easier.
>
> —DELTA CEO ED BASTIAN

The bulk of the information shown at the airport is unnecessary for an individual passenger. Innovations and trials like PARALLEL REALITY™ will ultimately tailor the airport experience to each customer through personalized navigation, information, services and offers. With the help of AI and algorithms, each customer can receive correct and real-time information even before they arrive at the airport.

The aviation industry has always been enthusiastic about innovation. After all, it is incredible that people can fly. Technology has been part of the solution and the experience from the start. Wouldn't this be the right time to also get the airports on board?

CASE: Helsinki-Vantaa Airport and Finavia

The Helsinki-Vantaa Airport has grown and developed in leaps and bounds. With twenty-two million passengers having passed through it in 2019, it is the largest airport in Finland. The Helsinki-Vantaa Airport is the shortest and easiest connection from Europe to Asia, which is evident in the number of international and connecting passengers from Japan, China, Russia and Hong Kong. In 2019, there were thirty-three airlines and fifteen hundred businesses in operation, and twenty thousand people working there.

Helsinki-Vantaa's development efforts and investments in the customer experience have paid off. It has received multiple international awards and accolades: the Best Airport in Northern Europe (Skytrax) in 2016 and 2018, and the best in the world (Travellink) in 2017. The SKYTRAX World Airport Awards are based on a survey of almost fourteen million passengers at more than five hundred airports. It evaluates the airport experience from check-in to commercial services, and from the security check to the departure gates. Most recently, in 2021, Airports Council International (ACI) presented

Helsinki-Vantaa Airport with the Airport Service Quality Award as the best of its size category (fifteen to twenty-five million passengers) in Europe.[62] The airport also received an award on its actions on hygiene during the 2020 pandemic.

> Smooth processes, high-quality services and expectations exceeding customer experience are the targets we work for every day at the Helsinki-Vantaa airport. It is an honor to receive recognition for this work and to be chosen as the best airport in Europe in our size category. I am particularly proud of the recognition regarding hygiene as we have invested a lot in health safety. **—ULLA LETTIJEFF,**
> Senior Vice President, Helsinki-Vantaa Airport[63]

Enabling the Entire Customer Experience Ecosystem

Butterfly Consulting has developed a customer experience management continuum for airports.[64] On one end of the continuum are airports that look after their statutory requirements, concentrating on basic processes, the maintenance of buildings and runways, and transporting customers.

At the other end of the continuum are airports that focus on managing the holistic customer experience: these airports are the cause of national or local pride. They think about their development programs customer-centrically (as the customer experience is part of their strategy) and they extend this to all their key partners. The best airports take responsibility for the customer experience, innovate, invest in employees and actively seek new sources of competitive edge and revenue.

Finavia, which has integrated the customer experience work into all operations and considers it as an integral and inseparable part of the overall passenger service and development work rather than a separate function, certainly belongs to the latter category. Building a uniform customer experience requires support, commitment and enthusiasm from the whole organization and all of its stakeholders. The community at Helsinki-Vantaa Airport includes hundreds of organizations. Every employee and business partner at the airport must believe in improving the customer experience in all daily activities, regardless of whether it is blowing snow from the runway or assisting passengers.

This is why a big part of customer experience work is to continuously increase the understanding of the customer experience and to keep the stakeholders accountable for the outcomes. When employees and business partners understand the importance of the customer experience through training, it is easier for them to make choices while on the job. To support every person in playing their part in creating a uniform customer experience, Finavia launched the Finavia Experience Academy, which provides mandatory training for all operators at Finavia airports. Putting every airport employee through the training is not only a big investment, but also a huge cultural change.

"At an airport, a comprehensive improvement of the customer experience requires structural changes and ensuring all the players of the airport community are engaged. The majority of the work is change management, employee and community experience management and integrating customer experience measures across all of our contracts," Timo Järvelä, Vice President Passenger Experience and Processes at Finavia, says.

When employees see how their own actions relate to the customer experience and everyone understands their own role in creating it, you are pretty far already. And service quality measures being part of every contract—whether cleaning, baggage handling or maintenance—ensure the customer experience remains at the center of all operations, is consistently put into practice and supported by the leaders.

One of Finavia's strategic goals is an exceptional customer experience. It has its own performance indicators on a companywide scorecard. The management team monitors the results of the global Airport Service Quality (ASQ) report performed at three hundred airports. The ASQ contains thirty-four metrics regarding services and satisfaction from the passengers' entire journey.

For Smooth Traveling

Since 2016, Finavia has defined what the customer experience means at Helsinki-Vantaa Airport. It is expressed by four pillars that provide terminology for everyone to use:

1. Feeling secure
2. Gift of time
3. Feeling refreshed
4. Feeling of Finnishness

The pillars are used to drive daily activities as well as large projects. For example, one of the guiding principles of construction projects is that new facilities are built explicitly for customers. The projects aim to combine the logistical point of view, which guarantees the functionality of the crucially important basic process, with the customer experience goals. As Finavia was building the expansion of the airport's southern wing, it reviewed the pillars of the customer experience together with the architects and designers: Will the plan support customers "feeling secure"? Will the expansion give the "gift of time" to passengers?

To improve its understanding of the customers, Helsinki-Vantaa Airport has segmented its customers based on their needs: there are pleasure-seekers, habitual travelers, caretakers and those who just wish to pass through the airport as quickly as possible.

The largest customer segment at Helsinki-Vantaa Airport are pleasure-seekers, often from Asia or Russia, who travel infrequently. A customer's segment can change during the trip or even based on the situation. Those on business trips often prefer to rush through: they jump from meeting to meeting during the day and hope for the queues at the airport to be as short as possible so they will make it to the flight on time. On the way to the plane, they may quickly grab something from the tax-free shop to bring home. However, sometimes their meetings end earlier than expected and they find themselves having two spare hours at the airport before boarding the plane. In this situation, the business traveler may become a pleasure-seeker and will expect the airport to meet their new needs and preferences.

"Here's another situation where we return to the functionality of the basic process," says Timo Järvelä. Whether it is a business traveler rushing to the gate or a vacationer in search of a new wristwatch, the basic process provides added value. In addition to processes, the other two of the

"Three Ps" of the airport customer experience are people and premises.

From Four Walls and a Ceiling
to an Intelligent Building and Operations

In its simplest form, an airport is a building. It has a floor, four walls and a ceiling. As at many other airports, the first digital solutions at Helsinki-Vantaa Airport, such as checking in, were implemented in the services of airlines. Digital check-in, over the internet or through the airline's own app, has significantly shortened the queues. Technology has also been present for a long time at the security and passport checks and digital gates. And new technology and innovation is rolled out to these crucial points of the passenger flow. For example, the new security gates that are being installed at Helsinki-Vantaa Airport are based on a completely new platform. Passengers will no longer be required to remove liquids from their bags, which makes the basic process smoother and more efficient.

But as one might guess, most of the magic of digitalization that allows the airport to run smoothly happens in the background processes. Data analytics enable a better understanding of passenger movements and digital solutions ensure that the premises are used effectively. "In addition to ensuring that customer experience is an integral and integrated part of all the visible operations at the airport, a lot of our work happens 'under the hood,'" concludes Timo Järvelä. "This is work that you do not see—you only realize it if something is not working well."

One of the biggest enablers is Finavia's Airport Operational Status (AOS) system that provides improved airport performance and predictability through shared situational awareness. In practice, AOS is a system that equips everybody working at the airport with a shared information and communications channel; it provides the staff with operation status, event feed and calendar, real-time flight data and passenger numbers, incident management and notifications. Bringing all the data together, making it accessible and sharing it with all the operators ensures everybody is viewing the same picture at any given time. AOS makes it possible to provide customers with a high-quality experience, and if needed it has the ability to react to unexpected situations.

Helsinki-Vantaa Airport is in the middle of a huge development program that continued throughout 2020 despite the Covid-19 pandemic. Once completed, the program will increase the overall terminal floor space by 45 percent and luggage handling and passport control capacity by 50 percent. The design of the expanded terminals is centered around developing the customer experience with the aim of improving service levels and creating completely new experiences. Digital services are central in outlining new service concepts.

One of the largest undertakings with regard to customers' experience of locality (Feeling of Finnishness) is a space where one can have a multisensory experience of Finland's unique, clean and diverse nature by digital means. In the Aukio extension, passengers can experience the Finnish nature with seventy meters of 360° LED screens, soundscapes and an interactive wall. It is widely known that nature has a calming effect, and this is one way to bring nature to the terminal. The Feeling Secure and the Gift of Time pillars are improved with dynamic signs that automatically switch to

Chinese or Japanese, for example, when a flight from China or Japan arrives.[65]

New Winds

As customers become more international, the expectations regarding a customer experience at a Finnish airport are changing. Despite the fact that customers expect the airport to have local flavor, they also want more services that suit their tastes. In 2017, the #LIFEINHEL campaign offered the opportunity for Chinese actor Ryan Zhu to stay at Helsinki-Vantaa Airport for thirty days. The campaign, which attracted a lot of attention in social media, aimed to gather information on how the customer experience at the airport feels to a young Chinese man and what services should be developed to improve the experience. Based on his experience, Zhu suggested increasing space, adding more dining options to suit Chinese tastes and including the ability to provide service in Chinese.

Now, Helsinki-Vantaa Airport has its own corporate page in the Chinese WeChat app, which combines WhatsApp-like messaging, a wallet, information sharing and a commercial platform. WeChat also has a ticket store, a taxi booking platform, a translation service and lots more. Finavia's presence on WeChat is part of the project to improve services and the customer experience of Chinese passengers.

At the same time, it is an excellent example of how even the most basic technologies and channels need to become more international and businesses must meet their customers where they are already with technologies and languages they understand. This has been taken into account at the airport:

at the tax refund point, Chinese customers can use Alipay, a Chinese mobile payment service. The airport has signs in Chinese, customer service attendants who speak Chinese and hot water points have been added. An electronic translation service helps with communication.

In 2020, Finavia launched the "Voice of the Customer" project solely aimed at developing its digital customer service and improving self-service opportunities. With the aim of creating a multichannel customer service system, the project will bring together interactions from multiple channels: website, social media and face-to-face.

The airport environment has many moving parts. New growth markets and international passengers bring their flavor to customer experience work. New technologies open up new possibilities. At an airport, as with other venues, the customer experience is ultimately defined by encounters and hence people. Even if the encounter happens with a robot (as with 5G robots currently in pilot phase in Helsinki-Vantaa), behind the robot is ultimately another human being. A robot needs human characteristics and expertise from actual people to be able to be of service in the encounter with a human. Digitalization smooths the development and running of basic processes at an airport, leaving more time and possibilities for encounters beyond the compulsory checkpoints.

HEALTHCARE

Digitalization carries lot of promise for the healthcare sector such as extensive cost savings and better care. An aging population with complex needs, limited healthcare resources and rising costs of care demands new innovations. As healthcare delivery networks are moving toward value-based care, digitalization is the only way to help the sector to provide better care at a lower cost.

Digitalizing patient records and electronic prescriptions have brought targeted quick relief in automating and streamlining healthcare processes. We are getting better and better at predicting illnesses using algorithms and giving diagnoses based on efficient data use, but a seamless patient experience remains a vision of the future.

Over the past few years, health delivery organizations have been focusing on digital care delivery to meet the unprecedented demand the Covid-19 pandemic caused for healthcare services. Care providers also needed to figure out how to protect the workers from the exposure to the spreading virus. Infected staff caused big challenges for already stressed healthcare systems. Unfortunately, we saw a growing number of burnouts among healthcare personnel. This obviously also led to weak patient experiences. The only focus was to survive the crisis.

The pandemic accelerated the adoption of digitally enabled care models. In a matter of days we needed to pass the traditional barriers like regulatory requirements and reimbursement models and change the way we provide care. Virtual care practices were set up around the globe in just days. Even when visiting a physician we couldn't escape conference calls; Microsoft Teams, Zoom and other virtual conference platforms were widely used to enable patient–clinician engagements.

The pandemic showed the need for timely and transparent information sharing. The ability to support employees and patients with relevant data became even more critical. For example, in the US, healthcare waste is extremely high, over 25 percent of the total healthcare spend. And the majority of the losses come from failures of care delivery or coordination due to lack of the right data.[66]

A Fragmented Patient Experience

Customers and patients are expecting the same level of digitalization and customer experience from their healthcare providers as from service providers in other industries. When navigating the complex ecosystems of different healthcare providers, the patient's journey is often getting lost!

Patients do not care about legacy patient data systems or a healthcare provider's internal silos. They look for engagement that is relevant, consistent and timely. They want an experience that travels among the variety of touchpoints and channels. The healthcare sector has a lot of catching up to do: when people were asked about their perception of communications and customer experience across seven sectors, only automotive and government ranked lower than healthcare![67]

The weak experiences have led to a consumerization of healthcare, the trend of individuals asserting more influence and control over their medical care. Patients are taking the lead from their healthcare data and defining their journeys to fit their personal priorities. To address this, nontraditional companies in retail (Amazon) Big Tech (Microsoft) and consumer package goods (Best Buy) are moving into healthcare to better meet consumer and patient needs. Consumerization of healthcare also changes the traditional roles in the industry and pulls the patient into the payer role.

In the most extreme circumstances, a customer experience in healthcare can be a question of life and death. However, usually it is about maintaining a continuous long-term customer relationship and offering personalized, timely and efficient care to prevent and treat illnesses. The growing number of chronic illnesses the world is seeing today requires lifelong relationships and new ways of treating patients outside the four walls of the hospital. Moving care from hospital to home requires innovative medical devices, trustworthy data transfer and new skills for healthcare personnel.

From Siloed Steps to Care Continuum

Most of the time, the patient experience is episodic: it is formed by steps (see figure 10). Some patient journeys are brief. And sometimes a patient is on "hold." For example, your foot hurts, you have a sore throat or you have other symptoms that make you decide to see a doctor. Sometimes you will receive care immediately; sometimes there will be days, even weeks, between when the symptoms start and when you see the doctor. During this period, you are on hold. After a while, you will meet the doctor, tell her about the symptoms, answer questions and get help in order to start the healing process. The same happens the next time you have an issue. The patient experience is customer-driven and reactive. The patient *is* the customer, and the customer experience occurs only when the patient has issues that she is not able to treat herself.

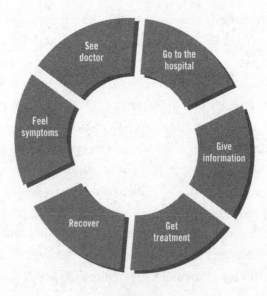

FIGURE 10

A typical reactive patient experience is full of short sequences of experiences.

However, treating illnesses proactively would be much cheaper and more effective. Most important, it gives a smoother experience to the patient. A successful patient experience is continuous, proactive, preventive and cohesive. Digitalizing healthcare aims at a holistic patient experience (see figure 11). Instead of expensive hospital care, the goal is for preventive measures and a relationship that extends beyond the time you are a patient. In a holistic relationship, the customer can access her health records regardless of place and time. In optimal situations, the patient should be able to contact healthcare professionals remotely, and the healthcare professionals should proactively communicate with the customer using data from remote patient monitoring devices. Personal support and advice are the keys to a good patient experience. Health is one of the most intimate areas of our lives.

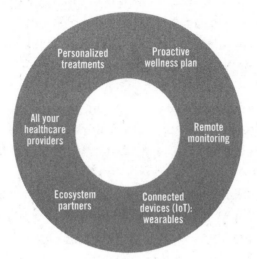

FIGURE 11

The patient experience of the future focuses on data, prevention, and continuous healthcare.

The patient experience should be in the customer's control regardless of whether the steps are created by an individual physician or multiple organizations. This sets big requirements for the background systems that will require seamless patient dataflows. This new way of treating patients is called "precision health."

Precision Health Thrives from Data

Health informatics ultimately enables precision health. Healthcare anywhere can only happen when smart technologies and digital tools are adopted enterprise-wide by clinical teams and patients. Precision health can be achieved when data is aggregated and presented at the point of care when the patient needs a diagnosis or care inside the hospital, and all the way home to monitor cure and recovery. Health informatics empowers clinical teams to deliver high-touch care throughout the patient journey.

Moving from monolithic systems to open, modular, often cloud-enabled platforms gives healthcare professionals real-time information to support their work. Advanced electronic medical records (EMR) systems can be complemented with data submitted by the customer and her devices. Consumerization of healthcare brings more and more wearables that measure different vital signs. By addressing alarming signals early, it is possible to address issues at an early stage and hence reduce the need for expensive and often more complicated healthcare.

Healthcare is moving toward more personalized service enabled by the efficient use of data. With efficient data transfer and global databases, diagnosing and treating illnesses will become more efficient when experiences can be shared virtually inside networks. The healthcare customer experience is becoming an always-on chain instead of episodic steps.

Patient Engagement Improves Experience

The patient experience has improved significantly due to healthcare's digital transformation. We still have a long way to go, but health IT technologies are getting better. Little by little, they are breaking barriers. Moving to holistic care and getting the patient engaged in her own wellbeing and care will help create not only a better care experience but enhance and direct scarce healthcare resources more efficiently.

Patient engagement means empowering patients to actively participate in their care, to take responsibility for their data, actions and health in a way that is appropriate for the individual, in cooperation with a healthcare provider. The purpose of strong engagement is to maximize health and quality of life by experiencing good care and effective clinical workflows, at reduced healthcare costs. The main aim of patient engagement projects is both cost savings and improvements in the patient experience.

Theoretically, a patient experience can happen without the patient actively participating, but by just receiving a service. A hospital or a clinic creates the experience and encourages the patient to actively engage to monitor and treat her own wellbeing. The outcomes of patient experience projects are typically measured by exceeding expectations (customer satisfaction), improving brand and increasing revenues to the care provider.

Typically, a good patient experience leads to a more engaged patient and better treatment results. To make holistic change we need a union of patient experience and patient engagement. A patient experience in healthcare is good if it keeps the patient healthy, engages the patient and gives her information about her health beforehand, which adds to the patient's feeling of being in control. Both the patient experience and enhanced patient engagement ultimately aim at the person's improved wellbeing and care results.

It is specifically the feeling of being in control of the situation that differentiates the retail consumer shopping at the grocery store from the patient visiting a hospital. Many times, the patient experience includes fears and feelings of vulnerability. Unlike grocery-store customers, a patient-customer often lacks the ability to choose the care provider from among a universe of alternatives, and the service is covered by the state or an insurance company. Also, comparing the service to other services is not always an option and might not even be possible due to individual care needs.

Patient Experience Helps to Improve Profitability

Healthcare operators and service providers must balance improving the customer experience and cost savings. Healthcare needs are infinite, but resources limited. In the most mature healthcare systems, like in the US, providers are moving to value-based care. In contrast to traditional fee-for-service (FFS) systems, value-based care aims to pay for value rather than volume by incentivizing providers and other stakeholders to improve health outcomes, while reducing the cost of care.

In reality, one does not need to choose between savings, better results and an improved customer experience. Investing in the customer experience has both revenue-increasing and cost-saving impact! According to a study by Accenture, US hospitals that focus on the patient experience instead of cost savings achieve a profit margin that is almost twice as high as hospitals that have been rated to have an average patient experience.[68] The study also claims that the correlation between a good patient experience and the hospital's profits will only increase in the future and that this will be the case with hospitals of every size and location.

Forrester Research made the same conclusion. According to its "The Business Impact of Investing in Experience" study, experience-driven healthcare providers are 1.6 times more likely to significantly exceed expectations in revenue growth.[69]

And the question is not just about increasing profits. A holistic and proactive patient experience helps with cost management. Waiting for problems and dealing with them once they have become worse is expensive and inefficient. Active engagement with the patient outside the hospital walls reduces costs. By shifting care to the home and using outpatient care, providers are saving costs and bandwidth. The biggest concern is the risk of readmissions, but with the help of modern devices and technologies that are providing advanced predictive models, this can be effectively avoided.

Digitalization and the Patient Experience

Digitalization has the chance to improve, change, shape and even completely renew the patient experience. The following improvements are helping to redefine customer experience in healthcare:

- *Innovations that improve gathering and analyzing patient and health data,* which enable and accelerate data analysis and improve preventive care. We will move from automatic reminders generated by a patient information system to the use of genome data, personalized medicine and biomedical imaging that rely on digital innovations. Doctors will leverage AI-screened and -refined health-, activity- and diet data from detectors, sensors and smart wearable devices.

- *Innovations that automate and personalize the customer relationship and interaction,* which enable faster and long-term care and monitoring. Patient portals, chatbots, distance care and virtual clinics with a remote video connection free up the doctor from spending too much time on basic questions and issues. That time can be spent on a personal and calm encounter with the person in need. In countries where the patient-to-doctor ratio is high or where people live mainly in rural areas, virtual clinics enable efficient care.

- *Innovations that enrich the hospital experience,* such as interactive TVs through which patients can order food, study and even invite their family and friends for a virtual visit. Through a virtual world, the patients can also "visit" their own homes and favorite places. CRM systems, as with hotels, help support the staff and enable service providers to respond to individual care needs and create more personalized service.

Efficient Gathering and Analysis of Patient and Health Data

Nowadays up to 90 percent of the patient information comes either from a patient information system or from the patient's "mouth." In the future, the vast majority of data will be gathered by detectors, sensors and smart devices. McKinsey Global Institute predicts that in 2025, 1.3 billion people will use a health and/or wellbeing monitoring device.[70] In some countries more than half of the population always carry some technology monitoring their lifestyle and health.

Even if deciding on a treatment is ultimately in the hands of a doctor, AI can help mine and refine data efficiently and take multiple factors into consideration in a short period of time. For example, in Finland, the Helsinki University Hospital together with the CleverHealth Network ecosystem has developed a mobile app to treat gestational diabetes. The solution, which leverages cloud services and AI, measures and stores blood sugar data, physical activity, nutrition and the weight of the expecting mother. By using machine learning, the patient's care and treatment is tailored to her personal risk profile and the AI generates predictions on the health of both the expecting mother and the baby.[71]

Digitalization also makes it possible for the patient to own, analyze and understand her own health data. The data doesn't need to be gathered separately, but it will be compiled from detectors, sensors and smart devices such as a smart mattress that measures sleep, or a smart watch or wristband that monitors physical activity. AI will take anomalies into account and send an alarm. It might even book an appointment with a doctor. Not just the increased data but also the ability to access it will revolutionize the customer engagement and enable the patient to be active in a long-term patient experience. After this, the patient experience will no longer be passive acceptance, but planning and creating together.

Better Customer Relationship and Innovative Interaction

In 2014, a McKinsey study reported than three out of four patients wanted to use digital services in healthcare.[72] And if there ever was talk of a digital engagement demographic divide, the pandemic has closed that gap: the use of digital to access healthcare service post-Covid-19 is at the same level across the age groups.

As with other areas of life, when consumers become accustomed to using digital services for healthcare, their expectations about improved care, personalization, efficiency, continuous interaction and a better patient experience increase. Consumers don't want to queue at the grocery and they certainly don't want to queue at the doctor's office; the patients would like care providers to provide an intervention at the right time, just as travel apps provide information about your destination at the right time.

> "Doctor Google" is the first place that young people as well as 80 percent of older people consult for a diagnosis.[73]

There are many great examples of the new interaction channels, operating models and innovations brought about by digitalization. Here are a few that are changing the way we approach care:

- Triage bots, check-in systems and robots speed up and automate the basic functions of a hospital visit, freeing up the workers to focus on more value-added tasks.

- Dynamic treatment plans and communication outside the hospital visits. Healthcare operators will be able to build a continuous relationship with their customers by creating additional services such as monitoring the data and reacting to alarms generated by smart wearable devices.

- The pandemic highlighted the importance of virtual clinics, which became the first point of contact in primary care.

- Applications that encourage health and wellbeing through gamification such as activity, nutritional and hydration apps.

Technologies That Humanize and Improve the Hospital Experience

Technology has brought convenience to hospital stays as well. The interactive TVs and tablets offered by some hospitals give patients the opportunity to order the food they want, adjust their room temperature, call their family for a virtual visit or even watch videos of their own operation. In the most progressive hospitals, the rooms look more like hotel rooms and the service is more suitable to a hotel than a traditional hospital.

The words "hospital" and hospitality" share a common root in Latin. Yet traditionally the experience has been quite different when you check into a hotel compared to a hospital. Yes, in both you need a bed and food but your expectations of the service when checking into a hotel are probably much higher than when signing into a hospital.[74] With digitalization, hospitals have begun to invest in the patient experience, service and a broader variety of alternatives.

Digitalization as a Background Force

In the background of the patient experience, digitalization helps to streamline operations but also supports healthcare workers with uniform patient information and new intelligent tools for patient care and communication. Hopefully in the future, healthcare workers will have personal virtual assistants to reduce the burden in their important work!

The efficiency and ability of healthcare workers to provide better service is supported by team-based and data-supported patient information systems that the workers can access regardless of time and place, perhaps even with a smartphone. Communication tools make it easier to keep in touch with other healthcare workers, patients, researchers and maintenance workers. This enables the minimization of time spent on searching for, updating and analyzing information, as well as communications, logistics and guiding resources to customer service, patient encounters and consultations.

As gathering and analyzing data become more automated, the doctor's ability to spend more time with patient work increases (currently it is only 27 percent of their working time). Technologies will free up time spent updating patient information and office work and enable doctors to focus on the patient.

As with other sectors, digitalization and technologies also change the role of the service provider, the doctors and other healthcare workers. In the future, a doctor's work will be more about consultation, motivation and/or coaching. The trend is the same as in the education sector: as the monopoly on information is crumbling, the work profile is changing, with a greater focus on customer service.

At the institutional level, hospitals will benefit from the efficiency opportunities brought about by AI. AI, video analytics and information processing all improve efficiency while simultaneously reducing the possibility for error. As with other organizations with a large number of workers and a reliance on infrastructure (building, devices), digitalization helps coordinate with complexity, increases flexibility (right staffing, different working methods, but also the possibility to move the care outside the hospital) and predicts maintenance and servicing needs, among other things.

CASE: Cleveland Clinic

Cleveland Clinic is a multispecialty healthcare system founded by four physicians in 1921. This organization has seen staggering growth: Cleveland Clinic employs more than 70,000 people and receives 8.7 million patient visits annually. It has 2.4 million unique patients globally. In addition to Cleveland, Ohio, the clinic has operations in Nevada, Florida and the United Arab Emirates, and it is building a new hospital in London. In early 2018, when Cleveland Clinic's CEO, Tomislav Mihaljevic, MD, assumed the role, he stated that the organization's ethical responsibility was to help as many people as possible.

Cleveland Clinic generates approximately $10 billion revenue annually.[75] The organization provides an example of a healthcare provider that has in recent years improved both the results of the care it provides and the patient experience, while simultaneously saving on costs.

Cleveland Clinic wants to be the best place for care anywhere and the best place to work in healthcare. It is globally known as the best cardiology and heart surgery provider and as of this writing has been recognized as the best in this field in the US for twenty-six consecutive years. In 2020–21, it was also recognized as the second-best hospital in the US.[76] The organization is known for its medical innovations, its use of technology and for pioneering the development of the patient experience.

The customer (patient) is at the center of all of Cleveland Clinic's activities. When Mihaljevic is asked for a single thing that best describes Cleveland Clinic's approach, he responds "Patients first" with no hesitation. This goal for the whole organization was first defined by the Clinic's previous CEO, Delos Cosgrove, MD, in the early 2000s. "Patients First" is how the patient experience is defined at Cleveland Clinic. This includes safe and high-quality treatment and customer satisfaction. "It is impossible to separate the patient experience from the quality of the care," says Mihaljevic.

> You know what is important to an organization by what they spend time on. Safety, Quality and Patient Experience on every agenda.
> —TOMISLAV MIHALJEVIC, MD,
> CEO, Cleveland Clinic

Patient Experience to the Center of Attention

Cleveland Clinic has had a reputation for providing good medical care for decades. Previously it focused on medical results. In 2009, then-CEO Cosgrove noticed that the customers weren't satisfied with the service they received or with the patient experience. "Patients came to us due to our expertise, but they didn't *like* us," Cosgrove has stated in several interviews.

Cosgrove decided to focus on the patent experience and nominated Cleveland Clinic's first Chief Experience Officer: the appointment was one of the first in the healthcare sector! The Chief Experience Officer brought the patient experience and its development onto the executive management team's agenda. In the first three years the focus was on getting the organization and the employees to commit to patient experience development work. Most important was that every employee understand what the patient experience meant and what role and responsibilities everybody had in providing it. The patient experience was defined as "everyone and everything people encountered from the time they decided to go to the Clinic until they were discharged."

The holistic approach paid off: Cleveland Clinic's ranking in the Centers for Medicare and Medicaid Services (CMS) patient satisfaction survey went from mediocre to the top 8 percent, among the 4,600 hospitals surveyed.

Customers Participate in Development Work

Since 2015, Adrienne Boissy, MD, MA, and her 120-person team have been in charge of the patient experience at Cleveland Clinic. The patient experience department focuses on consulting on initiatives, gathering and analyzing data on the customer experience and supporting and sharing exemplary projects. Just like at Finavia, most of the customer experience work involves increasing customer-experience awareness with the organization and employees, innovation and communicating about the importance of the issue throughout the organization. This work is supported by "patient experience champions" in every part of the Clinic who look after the uniformity of the customer experience across the diverse and broad organization.

During its first twelve years, the customer experience work has evolved. It has become a part of all operations.

Customer experience initiatives, large and small, are implemented together with customers. Sometimes seemingly small things can make the hospital experience more human and hence improve the patient experience. One example are the hospital gowns, designed in 2010, specifically for Cleveland Clinic by Diane von Furstenberg. Unlike most hospital gowns in the US, these cover your backside! Another great example are all the efforts made during the Covid-19 pandemic to allow patients to connect with their families. These efforts ranged from a caretaker holding an iPad to enable a patient to FaceTime her loved ones to installing glass walls so that patients could safely celebrate birthdays with their families.

Sometimes the initiatives are large, requiring internal sales efforts so that new kinds of ways of operating are accepted by all employee groups. An example of this is the will for the customer feedback to be transparent. All hospitals in the US participate in a patient survey by the Hospital Consumer Assessment of Healthcare Providers and Systems (HCAHPS), which has been designed and is governed by the Centers for Medicare & Medicaid Services (CMS). The survey explores patients' opinions and views about the care they received at the hospital. The results are public and can be found at medicare .gov/hospitalcompare.

In addition to the survey, Cleveland Clinic has decided to publish and make public all the reviews and feedback patients give about the doctors. The review entails an overall score and four subcategories: listening, respect, understanding of the patient's medical history and time spent with the patient. It also includes reviews on the Chief Experience Officer, which are public for everyone to see! A customer's recommendation is considered the greatest praise and compliment.

In the beginning of 2018, as Cleveland Clinic's new CEO, Tomislav Mihaljevic held his first "State of the Clinic" presentation. He announced the establishment of the "Caregivers First" organization as one of the new initiatives. At the end of the day, the patient experience and wellbeing, employee commitment and looking after the organization's resources are the factors that enable the business to grow and increase revenues. If one of the pillars fails, the others will suffer.

In recent years, many other large firms such as General Electric have appointed a leader in charge of the employee experience. "We are all here to look after patients, but we won't succeed if we don't also look after ourselves and our actions. My job as the chief executive is to look after the people who look after our patients," says Mihaljevic.

Technology and the Customer Experience

Mihaljevic believes that digital technology will enable smarter and more affordable care and a better patient experience. "The majority of our future plans rely on digital platforms: telehealth, data analysis and artificial intelligence," he says. Digital tools have enormous potential in making life easier for patients and reducing time spent waiting. "Embracing Digital" is one of the strategic goals for the Clinic.

Before the pandemic, there was a perception that the healthcare community was digitally divided and that the industry, which is overall more focused on the elderly, did not need to move to digital as their primary audience was not digital. Covid-19 highlighted the importance of the ability to pivot to digital-first engagement and the use of digital tools to screen and onboard patients.

Cleveland Clinic had been investing in telemedicine service for years. Three years before the pandemic, it was Cleveland Clinic's highest growing service with twenty-five thousand patient appointments in 2017. Express Care Online is a mobile application through which a customer can have an appointment with a doctor remotely using their smartphone, tablet or computer, either via booking an appointment or when they want to. Covid-19 increased virtual appointments from 20 percent to 70 percent in some parts of the organization. This means more than one million virtual telehealth visits were conducted in 2020! And patient satisfaction for telehealth is high: up to 90 percent of patients would be happy to have another virtual appointment.

Moving beyond simple phone calls, physical visits and notes in electronic patient records, the demand, use and satisfaction of telemedicine offers a perfect opportunity for Cleveland Clinic to reimagine the role digital touches play in patient care: where do telemedicine and digital technology overall complement the traditional methods of care and where do they offer a totally new way of reaching out to patients, offering personalized experiences, wherever they are and engaging with them daily? During Covid-19, the Clinic set up a system to digitally connect with Covid-positive patients on a daily basis and giving them a feeling of being cared for even outside the hospital.

In 2017, Cleveland Clinic signed a five-year cooperation agreement with IBM. The cooperation is about more efficient gathering and use of data and improving the work with patients. One of the most interesting areas for cooperation is cognitive information processing: using IBM's Watson in hospital operations, doctors make better and faster decisions; it has even changed the way researchers review cancer diagnoses and treatments.

The data available in healthcare is growing rapidly, and artificial intelligence helps identify patterns and can process massive amounts of data long after humans have exhausted their capacity or slowed down notably. AI is like a new decision support network and background support of the patient experience, helping minimize chances for mistakes and omissions.

While technologies, AI and machines do their part, the doctors can focus on human contact, relationships and patient interactions. This improves the doctor's role as a provider of personalized care in a completely new way. It is technology that enables Cleveland Clinic to make treatments and the patient experience more human. As Adrienne Bossy has stated, "We must digitize moments that can be and humanize moments that must be."

To enable and support caretakers to develop ways to maintain the relationships and making digital to feel human, even with virtual appointments, Cleveland Clinic developed a *Digital Health Playbook*.[77] Mihaljevic wants Cleveland Clinic to stay at the lead of innovators and find new applications for improving the customer experience.

Just as with other sectors, understanding the patient experience should begin with understanding the customer's hopes and needs. So far, digitalization in healthcare has focused largely on processes and the efficiency of the institutions (hospitals and clinics), but not very often on the customer's needs. However, digitalization provides an excellent opportunity to create a better patient experience as well as innovations to maintain and improve healthcare and minimize human errors.

All of this requires different parties—from researchers to doctors to data analysts—to cooperate. As discussed earlier, the single factor that most limits leveraging the benefits of digitalization is the lack of expertise. Diversity and different skill profiles should be actively searched for and encouraged. Having IBM at Cleveland Clinic campus is not a coincidence!

The founders of Cleveland Clinic had a clear vision to offer outstanding patient care through cooperation, compassion and innovation. This vision, centered around the customer experience, combines organizational processes and culture (cooperation), human touch (compassion) and digital (innovation). This has proven to be solid despite the fact that it was established at a time well before the term "customer experience" was invented!

EDUCATION

We cannot teach our kids to compete with the machines who are smarter—we have to teach our kids something unique. In this way, thirty years later, kids will have a chance. Education is a big challenge now—if we do not change the way we teach thirty years later we will be in trouble.   —JACK MA,
Alibaba founder and Executive Chairman

Even before the pandemic, the education sector was transforming. For the past decade, if not longer, digitalization and technology have been changing the society and the jobs for which schools and teachers are preparing their students. If anything, the pandemic accelerated the speed with which digitalization is transforming schools, education systems and the role of teachers. In the spring of 2020, schools needed to switch to remote learning for millions of students in an incredibly short time frame. Some institutions were ready and able to deliver remote learning immediately, while others struggled and sent printed packs of homework to their students. Parent–teacher meetings were conducted over Zoom, notifications and invoices were sent electronically, student recruitment campaigns virtualized and graduation parties at the end of the academic year were celebrated online.

Moving to digital learning made 2020 busy for EdTech companies: whether they were offering apps and solutions for education, for home schooling parents desperate for tutoring help or for those upskilling their workforce. In 2020, we saw large companies like Google and Microsoft doubling down on education, and EdTech start-ups collected $13.3 billion in global venture funding (compared to $4.7 billion in 2019).[78] Kahoot!, a Norwegian educational gaming company, reported 1.5 billion participating players in 2020 alone and Microsoft Teams is reported to have been used by 100 million students.

As the pandemic continues to impact our everyday lives, students' expectations of the future in education and the student experience continue to evolve: most institutions report that student surveys clearly indicate that students expect hybrid learning going forward. Not just as a continuation of the policies in place during the pandemic, but as a permanent approach. Students appreciate the flexibility that remote learning offers, and the increased accessibility provides a needed opportunity for those located far from cities or universities, working or parenting. Learning basic courses online and focusing the time on campus on social networking, group work, career counseling and interaction: what's not to like?

As digital natives, the most recent generation has grown up with intuitive technology and has learned to receive personalized services. Similarly, their expectations of "service" at school follow the same pattern: they expect experiences that are personal, convenient, quick and consistent. They want teaching and mentoring at the right time, tailored to their individual needs and prior knowledge.

Learning Skills for the Future

A teacher stands in front of a class for forty-five minutes at a time or more. They speak, write on the blackboard, take a short break and continue speaking. Students sit still and listen or work quietly. Progress and success are measured by standardized tests that assess the amount of knowledge memorized, subject by subject. This experience is offered to students in classrooms where desks are arranged in rows facing the teacher. This may sound familiar, but does it sound like a thrilling customer experience?

After school, many young people play games online in teams formed of players around the world. The game gets increasingly more difficult as the players progress. Creative problem-solving skills, critical thinking, the ability to work as a team and communication and language skills are required to be successful. These are the same skills that since 2016 the World Economic Forum has consistently reported to be among the top ten job skills for the future. So, which better prepares young people for the future and the real world: school or games?

| | Which better prepares young people for the future and the real world: school or games?

In Amsterdam, two nine-year-old boys are creating traditional paper posters about the capital cities of Europe at school, while spending weekends building *Minecraft* worlds and add-ons that they can also sell in the game to other players. An MBA student in London is finalizing her coursework on customer journeys by writing it down in a Word document (the only accepted format), while designing mobile apps as a side hustle. An autistic young man in Italy failed in every writing exam at school but flourished at the university when he was given alternative ways to express himself and is becoming a talented digital artist. Examples like these can be found everywhere!

In the same way that digitalization is transforming the retail sector, the hospitality industry and the manufacturing of goods, it is also shaping education. The way we work, the way businesses operate and the skills needed in society are radically different from what they were before. In the past, individuals needed to perform clearly predefined tasks in factories or offices. Today, however, many of these employees are required to process, combine, produce and relay information.

It is necessity to be able to think broadly, be creative and work in collaboration with a multifaceted and multicultural network.

As the world changes, the pressure for transformation in schools and in teaching grows. Many countries have already made or are currently making changes to their curriculums: giving digital skills the same emphasis as literacy and numeracy, emphasizing the importance of learning transferable skills and thinking about learning and the learning experience holistically.

Increasingly, businesses are treating the customer experience as a key pillar of their strategy. Could education institutions learn something from the improvement of the customer experience and its effects, not on economic success, but on learning outcomes? If so, what does this mean for the student experience and the learning experience?

Is a Student a Customer?

When discussing public services, the individual receiving services is traditionally called "a beneficiary" or "a citizen." You can find these terms in many education policies as well. Both words have a connotation of passivity and unification. And they surely do not position a student as a customer.

In countries where private schools and higher education institutions are common, customer-centricity and customer experience are familiar and more often used among educators. Parents paying for the education of their children and students with high tuition fees have greater expectations regarding quality and results. The reputation of a private school or university is a key differentiator and has a significant impact on the institution's ability to keep its current customers and attract new ones—just like businesses in other industries.

However, the student experience is a relatively new service in many public schools and even in academic research. For a long time, the institutions hid behind test scores or post-degree employability statistics, ignoring the experience during the actual education. Even though teaching is a service that teachers offer, many teachers do not consider themselves service providers whose role is to produce the best possible customer experience for their students. Neither does the feedback provided, based on good or bad experiences, impact the result or the future of the institutions directly, at least not in the short term or in a significant manner.

However, digitalization and the opportunities it brings is increasingly pushing the student experience to the top of the development program lists at schools and universities. In 2016, well before the pandemic, in a study conducted by Harvard Business Review Analytics Services, 80 percent of education leaders believed that digitalization would change the education sector.[79] They also believed that the greatest motivation for digital investments is the desire to improve the students' (customer) experience.

At the time of writing this book, the dust from the pandemic has not properly settled yet and students are still learning from home in most parts of the world. But if anything, 2020 has demonstrated the need for holistic improvements to the student experience: from access to digital tools to pedagogy and learning design and from student wellbeing to online classes. Student experience is not something that happens only on campus or in school, but more often than not it starts online, and the digital components follow the students throughout their time in the school.

Learning Experience at the Heart of the Student Experience

For decades, learning has for the most part been thought of as a cognitive process. As the term "customer" creeps into educational planning and development projects, we should consider what exactly is the (customer) experience of learning and what does a good learning experience mean for students. Is it to have a good time at school? Is it to learn as much as possible? Or maybe it is about achieving predefined learning objectives? Can the typical definition of a customer experience be used in the education context? Could we imagine a curriculum being built around customers and an understanding of their needs?

Mihaly Csikszentmihalyi, a well-known psychologist and professor, defined a good learning experience as the moment when a student is completely "sucked in" to what they are learning.[80] At this particular moment, learning massively intrigues the student and she is completely focused on working toward the objective. Csikszentmihalyi described this state as "flow." In a flow state, students work solely thanks to the pleasure that the task at hand brings them. Flow is when a student's skills and the task at hand are in perfect balance. This state is found in a channel between anxiety and boredom (see figure 12).

In short, a perfect learning experience is achieved when the student makes progress by pushing her own skills to the limit. Interaction with the teacher and other students plays a key role. Every student has a different skill level, ability to self-regulate and capacity to make independent decisions. Active student involvement, enabling students to achieve flow state and providing an optimal learning experience are built upon a service provider's (i.e., a school's or a teacher's) ability to offer personalized experiences to each student. The experience is influenced by both the environment in which the experience is offered (school) and by the service provider (the teacher in particular).

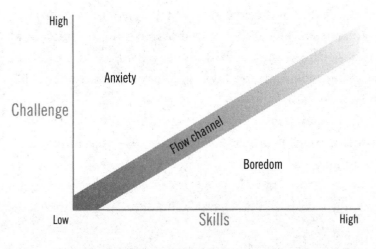

FIGURE 12

The ideal learning experience is the balance between existing skills and the level of the challenge at hand.

Learning Environment—Stage for the Learning Experience

Until just a few years ago, it was rare to see a classroom or a learning space that was not organized with rows of desks in a traditional fashion. Furniture remained in the same place from year to year with students occasionally changing where they sat.

New studies confirm that classrooms that support the development of learning experiences for students considerably influence their commitment and motivation. So today, when building new classrooms and physical learning spaces, the aim is to make things flexible so that the learning environment is suited to various types of tasks and students. For example, Lekolar-Printel in Finland has developed a classroom solution that is built around different learning situations: storytelling, discussion, doing, thinking, moving and energizing. The acoustics of the classroom are designed to minimize unnecessary sensory stimulation that may shift attention away from learning, and each student can influence their own learning experience by choosing a learning environment that suits them best.

When building new schools and campuses, it is also possible to seamlessly integrate technology in different spaces. If building a completely new school is not possible, one can start the change by redesigning an experience laboratory, for example—a space that changes and develops with the learning experience.

What about virtual learning spaces? Can we design and provide good learning experiences online? How much impact can the school or the teacher have on the experience delivered virtually, when ultimately the student needs to ensure the appropriate learning environment and take much more ownership of their learning by asking questions, taking part and keeping the conversation going? With the physical distance between teachers and students, can digital technology help keep students engaged and motivated and build the experience they need?

It might not be as easy as face-to-face; we may need more practice developing those virtual learning experiences. Since the start of mainstream remote teaching, student engagement has been one of the main challenges. The Economist Intelligence Unit reported that 60 percent of higher education faculty experienced a drop in engagement and 70 percent of faculty doubted their ability to deliver high-value learning experiences.[81]

But not at every institution! Take Florida State University (FSU) and its "Campus Reimagined" initiative as an example.[82] "Campus Reimagined" is offering personalized experience for forty thousand students. For example, a professor of an entrepreneurship class recorded one hundred six-minute-long, on-demand lessons. Students, using the custom app on their devices, voted for the class content for that specific day, giving them an opportunity to direct the course of study: turning the expected course syllabus into a colorful, non-linear gameboard.[83] Real-time polling with devices and prompts for video observations are examples of the ways Professor Bill Lindner enhanced student engagement and was able to provide an innovative and fun learning experience.

Teacher: The Experience Designer

Both in the physical and the virtual learning environment, the teacher is the ultimate experience designer. Whether in the classroom, online or hybrid, the role of the teacher is to guide her students, inspire thinking and support collaboration. Teachers are coaches, enablers and facilitators. As there are many ways to learn, there are also many ways to teach. A successful teacher enables each student to achieve flow, receive timely support and gradually develop independent learning skills. The learning experiences are formed through cooperation and interaction between a teacher and a student as well as among the students.

In K–12 classrooms, there are often twenty or thirty students and one teacher in a learning environment. At universities, the lectures can host hundreds of students! Digitalization enables transitioning from collective to individual learning—the learning experience can be tailored to suit each student and provide teachers with real-time information on the progress of each student.

For students, digital tools and content are a natural part of the learning experience. Some of the technology is student-facing. Its aim is to increase performance and the inspiration to learn. Depending on the school, students either have their own devices (school-owned or brought in by the student), use shared devices or work in computer labs. These devices are used for activities such as searching for information, completing quizzes, writing and participating in digital projects.

However, the biggest advantage of digitalization comes from its ability to support personalized learning. Immersive reading solutions support students of all reading levels and those who have difficulty reading or writing due to learning disabilities. Adaptive learning technology also identifies each student's particular strengths and weaknesses. On the back end, AI monitors students' development while analytical tools provide teachers with detailed information on students' progress and motivation in real time. This enables teachers to plan a personalized learning experience to support each student.

CASE: Catholic Education Western Australia

Catholic Education Western Australia (CEWA) offers a dynamic and student-centered education to 77,000 students in 164 schools across Western Australia. Eighteen percent of school-aged children and young people in Western Australia attend a school managed by CEWA. Maintained by the Catholic Church, CEWA's strategic goal is to develop each child holistically by focusing on their academic, spiritual, social, physical and emotional skills.

CEWA's objective of holistic development and improvement of learning results is largely supported by its digital strategy. The digital transformation started in 2016 with the "LEADing Lights" program that aimed to "empower all of us to reimagine the way we teach, learn and serve in order to deliver world-class learning experiences." Before LEADing Lights, every CEWA school had its own digital platform, tools and databases. The key idea of the new strategy was to bring the schools together and make use of a single, comprehensive digital platform across the entire school network and provide all staff and students with single credentials to access an integrated suite of tools and services within this platform.

For three years the LEADing Lights program improved learning experiences and created personalized digital learning ecosystems through a series of digital transformation projects, system-wide changes and the use of an end-to-end digital platform. Now digital is a fully integrated part of all operations and work at CEWA. With an evergreen industry-standard platform in place, teachers and students actively engage with the tools and in a culture that values collaboration and open dialogue.

The Student Experience—
Personalized Learning, Anytime, Anyplace

CEWA enables personalized learning regardless of time or place. It supports close collaboration and communication between students and teachers, as well as among peers.

For students, digital tools with analytics are an essential yet invisible part of their everyday school experience. Digitalization in itself is not important, but rather the possibilities it provides. The student portal is a cloud service that connects the academic and personal goals, tools, a peer network, homework and wellbeing status. Through the digital platform, students can monitor their own progress, take responsibility of their learning and network with their classmates and teachers. Through virtual school, students have the opportunity to participate in courses that their own school doesn't offer.

Students can use any device to access the portal. They only need to sign in once to get access in and out of school. The portal provides suitable tools for research, teamwork, coursework, evaluation and presentations.

Based on AI algorithms and peer recommendations, the platform provides students with personalized course and learning material recommendations. Each student is presented with materials and tasks that are of an ideal level of challenge, enabling them to reach the flow state and optimal learning. Progressing at the right pace also helps each student to "learn how to learn." Data and analytics help with learning paths and forecasts, allowing teachers to address potential problems early on. Simultaneously, students' particular areas of interest can be supported efficiently.

The strategy around data and analytics for 2021 focused on providing a single golden learning record for every student. Leveraging world-class data tools, artificial intelligence and student academic data, the recommendation engine builds a "golden" learning profile for every student. The data engine uses programmed logic to identify data across different legacy and cloud data sources containing student learning data and pulls it all into a single profile. The new golden profile spans the entire academic career of every student. These connected profiles improve the AI models in the platform to provide better projections of future student performance and recommendations for improvement.

> The data that's now available through the platform into classrooms and into schools and the wider System means that we can get early insights into students to measure and chart their learning information so that they're in the best possible conditions to fulfil their learning potential. It's something that only a few years ago we could have dreamt about, but not thought possible. —DR. EDWARD SIMONS,
> Director of Governance,
> Strategy and Digital Technology, CEWA

A good learning experience is achieved when students feel safe, when learning progresses at the right pace and students receive the necessary and appropriate support from teachers and the rest of their support network such as mentors and other students. The importance of safety extends to the digital world as well. A big part of the digital strategy is to provide a safe and secure digital learning experience within a school and across the schools. Because educators at CEWA better understand how the digital platform is secured, it provides more opportunities to teach and learn not only intraschool but also interschool across the CEWA platform. One of the key drivers is being able to connect learners with experts on any subject or topic, even if the topic is not taught at the local school.

Increased opportunities to collaborate and network outside a student's own classroom have enhanced the feeling of inclusion and encouraged finding one's own place as well as finding a community. The digital platform includes educational content, but above all else, it supports cooperation between individuals and the creation of shared experiences and results. For this reason, the teacher's role remains crucial, even in a strong, digitally supported learning environment.

The Teacher Experience—an Opportunity to Focus on Creating Innovative Learning Experiences

In CEWA schools, teachers consider themselves learning experience designers who modify learning circumstances and context for each student. Digital platforms and tools provide teachers with the opportunity for a new type of teaching and experience planning. The teachers' portal supports and guides teachers' daily activities as well as tasks in the classroom. Planning of the learning experience focuses on developing the classroom culture, shaping the physical learning environment and, most important, interactions with students.

One digital platform and a single sign-in to all systems enables efficient workflows and gives visibility to data. Streamlined and standardized reports speed up routine tasks, such as registering absences. For example, upon entering her classroom, a teacher uses a tablet to check who is present. In the background, analysis tools study potential recurring absences and share this information with the relevant teams and individuals. Consequently, the teacher is left with more time for teaching, mentoring and interacting with students.

As videoconferences, videos, podcasts, interactive presentations and websites enable new types of learning experiences, teaching no longer needs to take place in a classroom. In early grades, technology enables game-based learning and subsequently provides the opportunity to monitor, analyze and develop what has been learned.

The information provided by the "golden learning profile," with the help of AI and efficient analytical tools, enables targeted student interactions. Teachers have real-time, detailed knowledge of the needs, progress and stumbling blocks each student may have. This makes it possible to use the time in face-to-face meetings to focus on the most important matters. Teachers also enjoy a complete academic profile of a student's learning from kindergarten and pre-primary to graduation, even as she transfers from school to school in the CEWA system.

The communication and teamwork apps make it easy to share ideas, projects and resources among teachers. Teachers' professional development is supported by a virtual learning platform that uses AI to profile progress and goals. AI suggests suitable courses and learning paths for teachers, just as it does for students! Additionally, each term, CEWA provides a virtual conference week for teachers. These virtual learning opportunities connected more than 11,000 educators across 975,598 square miles (three times the area of Texas!) to learn from one another in 2021 alone!

Experience Is Built Through Meaningful Interaction

CEWA is one of the world's leading school systems in terms of leveraging cloud services, artificial intelligence and analytics to create student experiences. Despite digital tools being the cornerstone of the strategy and a part of everyday activities, it is good to remember that building the infrastructure and offering a digital platform is only the first step in creating a good student experience. Good experiences and, subsequently, good learning results are formed in the interaction and the social learning environment between teachers and students.

Building on the foundation the LEADing Lights digital transformation project provided, CEWA is currently working to improve four key areas to support student learning: expanded analytics capabilities, interschool engagement opportunities, expanding digital networking capabilities across the state and improving data security.

The recent increase in virtual learning experiences across the state highlighted the need to provide tools in the social and emotional learning (SEL) space. AI in applications within the digital platform was aligned to existing wellbeing frameworks used in schools. Wellbeing specialists and experts work together with teachers, school leaders and staff to design learning experiences with the wellbeing of the students and staff in mind. Quick pulse checks are woven throughout the platform, allowing students and staff to say how they feel about their day, their school, their current workload/assignments and their peers. Teachers discuss with their students how they feel, the pressures of school or life and how that may or may not affect their daily activities. The Visible Wellbeing program at CEWA guides leaders and teachers in how to use wellbeing and other data collected about a student to improve classroom and school learning experiences.

Just like improving the customer experience in business, improving the student experience is a comprehensive project that requires innovation, change management, commitment and new modes of operation at all levels. It is important that improving the student experience is included in the strategy, and that each school and all the stakeholders are part of the change. And like the example of the SEL space, a changing environment and changing needs also help guide the focus areas.

From the start, the digital transformation at CEWA has aimed to get all the stakeholders in the school system involved and to make the most of this comprehensive change. For school leaders, digital learning environments provide new data points to build learner and class profiles based on the models and theories used in their educational planning. School administrators are happier with a digital platform that supports and automates operations such as processing invoices, enrolling students, monitoring grades and keeping attendance records, allowing administrators and teachers to focus on student wellbeing. Digital tools reach parents, too, by offering them the opportunity to monitor their child's development in real time as well as offering an efficient communication channel with the school.

Shift to a More Student-Centered Experience

For any business, the success of the customer experience is rated by the customer. In schools the final say is with the student. A good learning experience has a huge impact on student wellbeing as well as improving learning outcomes. Even though, in schools, a good customer experience does not affect short-term revenues or customer attrition, the experience plays a significant role in motivating students to learn, and ultimately impacts their future success.

Digital investments are increasingly focusing on the student experience, and student experience is more often than not found in the strategy of educational institutions. Digitalization creates new opportunities to learn and teach, but it also strengthens and clarifies interaction between teachers and students by producing real-time information on the development, successes and challenges of students. Students receive personalized teaching, recommendations and guidance. And thanks to AI, potential challenges can be predicted.

During 2020 and 2021, no educational institution was able to avoid going digital, and even the most digital-resistant have found themselves using technology to teach. There is no going back! For a whole generation of students, the global pandemic has shown that learning can happen in a variety of environments; teachers are there to help, but the ownership of learning is with the students. Their expectation of being able to leverage the best of both worlds (campus life and virtual) is widely documented.

While the majority of the education community is still in the midst of dealing with arguably the biggest-ever disruption to learning and it is almost impossible to predict what the future of education looks like, the success stories from around the world like CEWA inspire other schools and universities to change and demonstrate that we are heading in the right direction.

5

FROM PLANNING TO ACTIVATION

Digitalization offers companies an unprecedented opportunity to make their business customer-centric. It brings new business opportunities, opens new markets and makes work more pleasant thanks to increasingly automated processes and new, interesting tools. Digitalization is all around us. During the pandemic it felt like our lives, work, education, purchasing and entertainment were only digital!

Change in the digital-first era is fast and at times hard to locate. Because many improvements brought about by digitalization happen "under the hood," they can be difficult to detect in corporate processes, culture and technology. At the same time, as consumers, we all can celebrate the tremendous progress in almost every sector as services improve and business transactions become easier. Customer information is available in more and more corporate systems, communicating in different channels is smooth, payments are processed without issues and new services that make life easier are in continuous development.

Surrounded with endless opportunities, the digital transformation journey can also feel exhausting. Digitalization requires continuous learning. Progress will continue to be fast in the future. You have to accept the fact that the world will never be fully finished! Therefore, it is pointless to start building solutions that are too heavy and difficult, even impossible to change in the future. Dynamism from organizational culture to IT systems helps businesses cope with changes in customer purchasing behavior, needs and expectations. Agility is the name of the game. Customer-centricity has become the most important driver for corporate success. Businesses that are able to change with their customers will succeed.

Everyone has surely heard the phrase "Well planned is half done." It has a hint of truth, but regrettably even good plans often remain in the drawer or planning takes way too much time and nimbler competitors are able make their moves to lure customers to their side. For developing the customer experience in the digital-first world, instead of "less planning," the guideline could be faster experimentation, enabled by new technologies, real-time monitoring and adjusting. Bad decisions can always be replaced with a host of new decisions. The most important thing is to get started and stay abreast of the progress!

> Well planned is half done. But only what's done is done.

But while moving forward quickly, experimenting with new approaches and staying in tune with the digital change, we should keep the following two things in mind. First, digitalization can't be a component that's pasted onto something. Developing a business should start with the customer. The customer experience should inform and even change the business strategy and the core corporate processes. It's more than just the interface visible to the customer or a single element along the customer journey. Taking digitalization into account in business is not a technology project. While we should not play down the importance of technology, an IT-driven initiative will probably fail.

Second, digital initiatives often fail because the starting point is copying competitors. A strategy or a solution copied from a competitor rarely brings competitive advantage, at least not within the same sector. Adopting some technologies, such as a messaging app in customer service, can certainly be a minimum requirement expected by customers that the business needs to fulfil. However, true digital customer-centric development starts much deeper, from the real needs of your customers and the core competitive capabilities and value your business is offering.

FROM THE DRAWING BOARD
INTO PRACTICE

Managing customer experience, digital or not, is holistic strategic management of the business. Customer experience is the cornerstone of the strategy for each business and organization discussed in this book: it sets the direction and mindset for developing each business and service. The words "customer" and "experience" can be found in the value statement and core promise of all the businesses featured as case studies in this book:

- Cleveland Clinic: *"You know what is important to an organization by what they spend time on. Safety, Quality and Patient Experience on every agenda."*

- Virgin Money: *"The strength of the business is our customer focused strategy."*

- Finavia: *"Our customer promise is 'For Smooth Travelling.' It means we will do everything we can to satisfy our customers."*

- Catholic Education Western Australia: *"We will reimagine the way we teach, learn and serve in order to deliver world-class learning experiences."*

As discussed earlier, developing the customer experience should start from the corporate culture, identifying and leveraging internal competencies, improving processes, strengthening brand and measuring outcomes. The tools for development can be found in new technologies. It is precisely rapid development of technology that has caused the customer experience to shift to:

- Processes that are expected to have increased efficiency, accuracy and integrability.

- Developing internal competencies as the foundation of the customer experience.

- Comprehensive and multisource measuring of the customer experience.

- Efficient use of technologies.

Customer-experience work always starts with the *customer*. The first question of all customer-experience work should always be: "How can we create a better experience for our customers and exceed their expectations?" The search for the answer begins with analysis based on data and deep customer understanding, but also creative thinking. One should not look only at existing solutions or examples. True success is not born out of copying.

OPTIMIZE PROCESSES

The integrity, efficiency and reliability of the process generating the customer experience is the next step of development work. A customer experience is born out of every encounter the customer has with a business or an organization. Today, more and more encounters take place digitally and with a machine.

An encounter doesn't mean just a direct interaction with a business or an organization, but it can be any operation or transaction, such as payment. Creating a holistic experience requires complete integration of the customer journey with all functions of the business, and often with its partners and experience co-creators as well. Both the customer journey and the business processes go across departmental and organizational boundaries, changing the dynamic between departments and individuals.

A business should first fix its basic processes: at the airport this is the customer making it from the terminal door to the departure gate on time; at the bank it is the feeling that the customer has her monetary affairs in order; at the grocery store it is availability of goods and ease of payment; and in healthcare it is foreseeing, treating and curing illnesses. If the basic process doesn't work, all the other initiatives aimed to improve the customer experience will fail or have no significance. The impact of digitalization and increased customer expectations should be considered carefully. What was previously a sufficient level of a basic process may no longer be enough. For example, previously customers were willing to wait, but now they are not.

Data, AI and other advanced technologies offer new ways to develop the basic process. The process becomes more efficient, error margins shrink and potential problems can be predicted efficiently. These days there are very few processes that don't rely on technology. That is why developing the business requires expertise in both technology and to the area where it will be applied. In the future, professionals from different disciplines and with different backgrounds, such as researchers, doctors and data analysts, will work in close cooperation with one another.

In developing processes, the following topics should be examined:

■ Your basic process that must be absolutely right.

■ The points of the customer process that are not currently smooth. What things do customers give the most feedback on, or at which point of the digital process does the customer leave?

* Steps that are unnecessary and could be removed to improve the customer experience. What steps could be automated? It is often easier to add than to remove.

* Information about and competence in new technologies to develop the processes.

ENSURE COMPETENCE AND A CUSTOMER-CENTRIC ORGANIZATIONAL CULTURE

The customer experience is closely tied in with the employee experience: to support the reimagination and optimization of the processes, investing in and increasing internal competencies and changing the organizational culture are crucial. Support from leadership and a commitment to customer-experience work are the first step. After that, the organization should focus on acquiring, developing and retaining the required competencies. Competencies can be hired, but in some situations partnering and forming ecosystems will be a more sustainable option.

Most of the time, the moment of truth for the customer experience is in the encounter between the customer and a staff member. Creating an employee-led experience is, or at least should be, strongly supported by data and analysis. Do make sure that you enable your employees to offer exceptional customer experiences!

In developing culture and internal competencies, at least the following should be examined:

- Does your business have a strong value statement emphasizing the customer? Does it also happen in real life? Values are easy to define, but they also need to be put into practice!

- Have the needs brought about by digitalization been identified and have they been considered in HR strategy and hiring? Don't forget diversity! It can be a good idea to acquire competencies from outside one's own sector or geographic area.

- Are the employees given enough resources to develop and create a digital customer experience? It is impossible without data and tools.

A strong, customer-centric culture ensures that not just competence but the willingness and ability to act customer-centrically is considered when hiring and promoting employees. Culture is also the common thread that guides decision making and ensures that the customer is at the heart and center of the investments, strategy, programs and initiatives.

SET SPECIFIC INDICATORS AND MEASURE THE RESULT

The state of the customer experience should be measured and monitored closely at all the levels of the organization, including the executive level. It is important that the customer experience is not left as a project for marketing, IT or any other single business unit, but that it is seen as an integral part of the organization.

The digital customer experience is closely connected with the core business, and the indicators should be set accordingly. This is why a scorecard measuring the customer experience alone will not give sufficient information on the situation and state of the business. A customer can "like" the experience provided by the business but buy from competitors. Purchase behavior is a better indicator of customer loyalty than a survey. A good example of this is travel portals. Not many people will admit they are real fans, but practice has shown that many customers do make their purchases via the portals.

As has often been stated, digitalization changes processes and purchase behaviors in ways that are not always easy to identify or even realize. Customers are not necessarily always able to say why and how they make their purchases. This requires the indicators to be set smartly so that the monitoring leverages several information sources. We may say that we prefer to use local, environmentally conscious providers, but in our busy day-to-day lives we end up becoming customers of the big multinational corporations because transacting is easier and faster. Or maybe we purchase local items on Saturdays when shopping at the farmers market, but the order our smart fridge makes is programmed based on availability and delivery options of the produce.

In developing indicators, at least the following should be examined:

- Are the indicators you use still valid, even if business is digitally transforming? Do they give versatile information on customer loyalty and purchase behavior? It's the customers' actions that count!

- Is the customer analysis based on data from different sources? The information should be available without delays. New technologies remove manual work and visualize information efficiently.

- Is compensation based on customer indicators? Remember the old rule: you get what you measure!

Leverage New Technology

The starting point of building a customer experience in the digital era is leveraging modern technology. It is impossible to offer customers dynamic, integrable services with old, rigid systems. The basic pillars of digital customer experience—automation and personalization—are both strongly based on leveraging new technologies.

Another significant change is increased speed. Customers expect efficiency not only from communications, but also from delivery and purchase processes. Being reactive is no longer enough. The best businesses in each sector can already offer proactive service. This sets a new standard for the other players.

Strong technology partners help not only to understand and leverage available technologies, but also to give access to new markets as the platform economy changes the earnings logic of sectors. Partnering is the best way to take cover from adverse changes.

In developing technology, at least the following should be examined:

- Have technologies been invested in sufficiently to offer a competitive customer experience? Remember that customer expectations increase constantly!

- Does the chosen partnership network offer enough information, expertise and alternatives to develop new customer solutions? Challenge your partners to present the best examples in different industries!

- Is technology-led innovation the responsibility of just a few, or is it part of the corporate culture? Ensure that basic skills grow and that everyone improves the customer experience as part of their work.

Even though the elements of developing the customer experience go hand in hand and repeat in the development cyclically, it is good to carefully consider required skills and resources needed when implementing different development initiatives. This should be done in the planning stage.

A good strategy is to break down large change projects into smaller parts so that the results and effectiveness can be measured in the short term. This is important to secure visibility, funding and support for the project in the future. And it's most important for getting employees committed. Quick wins help to build a positive atmosphere, and successes increase faith in what is to come. You can seek examples from the leading companies around the world, but please remember that copying others is not helping you to impress your customers in a differentiated way.

We wish you all the best for the exciting journey of seeking new ideas to get closer to your customers! Hopefully you have gotten some ideas from this book already. Good luck!

6

THINK BIG! NOTEBOOK

On the following pages, we have gathered together
THINK BIG! thought exercises. The purpose is to help you
give structure to the ideas you may have gotten while reading
this book.

Make notes on ideas, thoughts and examples. These will
help you get started. Shake yourself out of the thought models you have become used to and think how you could really
change your customer's experience of your service or product by leveraging the possibilities of digitalization. Maybe you
will come up with something no one else has been able to
leverage yet. The best ideas are often simple!

Don't constrain your thoughts by fixating on problematic
parts. A couple of years ago no one would have thought we
would be jumping out of a cab without paying or staying at
someone else's home rather than a hotel when traveling.
What's the next thing that desperately needs a reform? Examine things through the eyes of a consumer. Often the things

that annoy us as consumers give us a tremendous opportunity to build new business.

It is probably time to update the old adage "Well planned is half done." The truth is that only a project that has actually been completed is really done. The biggest challenge with development projects related to digitalization is completing them. Consider how you can make your ideas actually happen.

Remember that most ideas focus on reshaping what already exists, even when the changes going on in the market would require real shaking of the existing structures. Therefore, THINK BIG!

#1 THINK BIG! If you were the customer of your digital service, what things would frustrate you? Think about how these could be automated or eliminated with the use of technology. Think broadly and try to avoid the most obvious answers!

#2 THINK BIG! What are the three technologies that you will test this year in developing the customer experience? In what elements could you be a forerunner and surprise your customers by offering something unique that others are merely planning? Remember that adopting the most common technologies alone will not yield a competitive advantage!

3 THINK BIG! What information would you like your business or organization to gather, analyze and apply to ensure a personalized service experience? Why? Your customer probably feels the same! Make a list of things you assume businesses already know about you based on your previous purchase behavior.

#4 THINK BIG! Instead of threats, challenge yourself to think about the opportunities digitalization offers. What is the biggest benefit of digitalization? Perhaps it could be going international, entering new markets fast or offering the most efficient customer service in the industry. Think of a strong digital vision for your business. How can you enable it to happen?

#5 THINK BIG! How can you network and partner to achieve gains of the platform economy? Who is the next likely reformer of your sector? What kind of network does your business have? Networking outside your own sector is also beneficial. The majority of success stories have started from disrupting sectors!

#6 THINK BIG! In your strategy, focus on the customer, not the competitors. As long as you have an excellent understanding of your customer's needs and you can react to them, you are ahead of your competition. Based on data, what are the five most important things to your customer? How do you ensure that they shine brightly as the guiding stars at your workplace?

#7 THINK BIG! How do you ensure that everyone develops processes, operations and products to become more customer-centric as part of their jobs? Customer-centricity is not a privilege of one team. Do you use new tools in order to gain new insights into customer data and hence develop the customer experience yourself?

#8 THINK BIG! If your customer could draw their customer journey themselves, what would it look like? How do you get closer to it? Start from the customer and design everything else after that!

#9 THINK BIG! Could you remove all the internal processes that do not contribute to a good experience? The customers' needs invariably change faster than internal corporate processes. What would happen if you gave up the old operating models? Which of the internal processes would go to the trashcan? Why?

#10 THINK BIG! Could you reward your staff based on customer indicators? Do feedback and compensation really incentivize seizing customer feedback, hopes and challenges or move them somewhere else in the organization? Frustratingly often, the customer is left going around in circles in the internal corporate processes.

ACKNOWLEDGMENTS | SANNA

Belinda, it is unbelievable how far a pact made in the English countryside can take us! I'm happy we embarked on this journey together and we have been able to talk about and write about customer experience together—something we both feel so passionate about.

Thank you, Microsoft Alumni Network, for your partnership with HarperCollins that gave us the opportunity to share our insights, experience, and leadership skills through this book.

I have been extremely lucky, throughout my studies and work life, to get to know an enormous number of superstars, many of whom have been supporting this book as well. Tom, Johanna, Cathy, Sunil—you have inspired and colored my writing yet kept its feet on the ground. The work you do each day is simply amazing!

Thank you, Kasperi, for daring me to explore new things and believing that everything is possible. Kasperi, Mum, Dad, Jupu, Anne, and Iris—you are my rocks every day: mentally, spiritually, and practically. I would not be here today writing this without you.

Aino and Anni, when you read this book in ten years' time, you will notice that neither did Mum nor the international experts know all the things that digital will transform and create. It makes me happy that I can live through these exciting years with you.

One of my all-time favorite sayings is from Benjamin Franklin: "Well done is better than well said." Well, the book is now done, but lots remains to be done with the digital customer experience.

ACKNOWLEDGMENTS | BELINDA

Writing a book is always an exciting challenge! *The Swipe-Right Customer Experience* is my fourth business book, but the journey still feels the same: same excitement, anxiousness, and flow when learning new things during the research period and hearing fascinating customer stories from different companies and industries. Every time the goal is the same, to inspire *you*, our reader, to get some new ideas and to THINK BIG!

Compared to all the previous books, this book is a very special one. This one would have never happened without my dear co-writer, *Sanna*. Her dedication, commitment, and inspiration got us where we are. The best moments in life are shared, and I will always be thankful for this one.

I would also like to express my appreciation to a company that I truly admire. Microsoft Alumni Network has been supporting us to make our dream come true. Supporting women in tech and female authors (there are more John-named guys writing business books than females!), they are making this world a bit more diverse. One step at a time.

It goes without saying that my deepest debt of gratitude is owed to my husband, *Lasse*. A working mom writing a book needs some flexibility from the whole family. In my case it's been a shared life experience with so many good conversations, debates, and observations. Lasse, your knowledge has been helping me to understand the technologies that are shaping our future.

Writing is fun most of the time, but sometimes challenging and occasionally nerve-racking. In those moments the support from the people around you is crucial. Thank you, my dear friends (you know who you are), Mom, colleagues. You all made this possible!

One chapter of my writing life has come to its end, but this is only the beginning of lifelong learning. There are always some new inspiring topics to explore and that keeps us moving. Until next time!

NOTES

Chapter 1

1. Mariel Soto Reyes, "Google, Facebook, and Amazon Will Account for Nearly Two-Thirds of Total US Digital Ad Spending This Year," *Business Insider*, December 3, 2020, https://www.businessinsider.com/google-facebook-amazon-were-biggest-ad-revenue-winners-this-year-2020-12?international=true&r=US&IR=T.
2. "2021 Digital Trends Predicts a Post-Pandemic Future," *2021 Digital Trends Report*, Adobe, n.d., https://business.adobe.com/uk/resources/reports/digital-trends-2021.html.
3. "The Future of Jobs Report, 2020," World Economic Forum, October 2020, https://www3.weforum.org/docs/WEF_Future_of_Jobs_2020.pdf.
4. Katie Jones, "Ranking the World's Most Valuable Brands," Visual Capitalist, January 30, 2020, https://www.visualcapitalist.com/ranked-the-most-valuable-brands-in-the-world/.
5. Dana Mattioli, "Amazon Changed Search Algorithm in Ways That Boost Its Own Products," *Wall Street Journal*, September 16, 2019, https://www.wsj.com/articles/amazon-changed-search-algorithm-in-ways-that-boost-its-own-products-11568645345.
6. "15,000+ Consumers and Business Buyers Weigh in on the Future of Customer Engagement," Salesforce, October 27, 2020, https://www.salesforce.com/news/stories/15000-consumers-and-business-buyers-weigh-in-on-the-future-of-customer-engagement/.
7. Steven Van Belleghem, "The Difference Between a Customer Journey and a Life Journey," *Steven Van Belleghem Blog*, September 8, 2020, https://www.stevenvanbelleghem.com/blog/the-difference-between-a-customer-journey-and-a-life-journey/.
8. James Allen, Frederick F. Reichheld, Barney Hamilton and Rob Markey, "Closing the Delivery Gap," Bain & Co., 2005, https://media.bain.com/bainweb/PDFs/cms/hotTopics/closingdeliverygap.pdf.
9. Ecommerce has already become A-commerce (automated commerce).

Chapter 2

1. "Gartner Forecasts Worldwide IT Spending to Grow 9% in 2021," press release, Gartner, July 14, 2021, https://www.gartner.com/en/newsroom/press-releases/2021-07-14-gartner-forecasts-worldwide-it-spending-to-grow-9-percent-2021.
2. "Global ICT Spending: Forecast 2020–2023," IDC, n.d., https://www.idc.com/promo/global-ict-spending/forecast.

Chapter 3

1. "Future-Proofing Via Experience Ecosystem Investment," Adobe Summit infographic, 2021, https://static.rainfocus.com/adobe/as21/sess/160710 81478190015z6K/FinalPresentationUpload/S854Future%20Proofing Via%20ExperienceEcosystemInvestment_1618980834262001n0Lx.pdf.
2. Malcolm Gladwell, "A Crisis Is a Terrible Thing to Waste," Adobe Summit, April 28, 2021, https://business.adobe.com/summit/2021/sessions/malcolm-gladwell-a-crisis-is-a-terrible-thing-to-w-s958.html.
3. Greg St. Martin, "Study: Some Online Shoppers Pay More Than Others," News@Northeastern, October 23, 2014, https://news.northeastern.edu/2014/10/23/ecommerce-study/.
4. "Fairness You Can Bank On," Accenture, https://www.accenture.com/us-en/case-studies/applied-intelligence/banking-aib?src=SOMS.
5. Moral Machine homepage, https://www.moralmachine.net/.
6. Tripp Mickle, "Google's Head of Responsible AI Explains How It Works," *Wall Street Journal*, May 11, 2021, https://www.wsj.com/articles/google-plans-to-double-ai-ethics-research-staff-11620749048?mod=djemalertNEWS.
7. "Leaders Wanted," Technology Vision 2021, Accenture, https://www.accenture.com/gb-en/insights/technology/_acnmedia/Thought-Leadership-Assets/PDF-3/Accenture-Tech-Vision-2021-Full-Report.pdf.
8. Eli Rosenberg, "'The Shed at Dulwich' Was London's Top-Rated Restaurant. Just One Problem: It Didn't Exist," *Washington Post*, December 8, 2017, https://www.washingtonpost.com/news/food/wp/2017/12/08/it-was-londons-top-rated-restaurant-just-one-problem-it-didnt-exist/.

Chapter 4

1. "US Ecommerce Grows 32.4% in 2020," DigitalCommerce360, n.d., https://www.digitalcommerce360.com/article/us-ecommerce-sales/.
2. Joan Verdon, "Global E-Commerce Sales to Hit $4.2 Trillion as Online Surge Continues, Adobe Reports," *Forbes*, April 27, 2021, https://www.forbes.com/sites/joanverdon/2021/04/27/global-ecommerce-sales-to-hit-42-trillion-as-online-surge-continues-adobe-reports/?sh=2083dd8050fd.
3. "US Ecommerce Grows 32.4% in 2020."

4. "Nike's Breakup With Amazon May Lead Other Brands to Call It Quits: analysts," S&P Global, January 6, 2020, https://www.spglobal.com/market intelligence/en/news-insights/latest-news-headlines/nike-s-breakup-with -amazon-may-lead-other-brands-to-call-it-quits-analysts-56193375.
5. "US Ecommerce Grows 32.4% in 2020."
6. "With Holiday Shopping More Digital Than Ever, Consumers Say They'll Spend More Money if They Can Message with Associates or Chatbots," LivePerson infographic, n.d., https://liveperson.docsend.com/view/w8k8 rpd89wx4idkj.
7. "Study Reveals the Complexity of Modern Consumer Paths to Purchase and How Brands Can Make Inroads," Think with Google, June 2018, https:// www.thinkwithgoogle.com/intl/en-cee/consumer-insights/consumer -journey/study-reveals-complexity-modern-consumer-paths-purchase -and-how-brands-can-make-inroads/.
8. Aaron Orendorff, "The State of the Ecommerce Fashion Industry: Statistics, Trends & Strategy," Shopify, March 29, 2021, https://www.shopify.com /enterprise/ecommerce-fashion-industry.
9. Richard Pallot, "Amazon Destroying Millions of Items of Unsold Stock in One of Its UK Warehouses Every Year, ITV News Investigation Finds," ITV, June 22, 2021, https://www.itv.com/news/2021-06-21/amazon-destroying -millions-of-items-of-unsold-stock-in-one-of-its-uk-warehouses-every-year -itv-news-investigation-finds.
10. "Discover the Kantar BrandZ Most Valuable Global Brands," Kantar infographic, n.d., https://www.kantar.com/campaigns/brandz/global.
11. "Annual E-Commerce Revenue of Alibaba from Financial Year 2011 to 2021, by Region," Statista, May 27, 2021, https://www.statista.com/statistics /226793/e-commerce-revenue-of-alibabacom/.
12. Thuy Ong, "Alibaba's Car Vending Machine in China Gives Free Test Drives to People with Good Credit Scores," The Verge, March 26, 2018, https://www.theverge.com/2018/3/26/17163478/ford-alibaba-cat-car -vending-machine-china.
13. "Tmall Partnership with Ford Gives Test-Drives a Tune-Up," Alibaba Group Facebook page, https://www.facebook.com/alibabagroupofficial/posts /1600301263419778.
14. "Alibaba Revamping Ladies' Rooms to Make Waiting More Fun," Alibaba Group, Facebook video, February 5, 2018, https://www.facebook.com /watch/?v=1548214908628414.
15. "Alibaba's Gross Merchandise Volume on Singles' Day from 2011 to 2021, by Region," Statista, November 12, 2021, https://www.statista.com/statistics /364543/alibaba-singles-day-1111-gmv/.
16. PWC's 19th Annual Global CEO Survey, cited in "Financial Services Technology 2020 and Beyond: Embracing Disruption," PWC, 2016, https:// www.pwc.com/gx/en/financial-services/assets/pdf/technology2020 -and-beyond.pdf.

17. Bain/Research Now Customer Loyalty in Retail Banking survey, cited in "Evolving the Customer Experience in Banking," Bain & Company, 2017, https://media.bain.com/Images/BAIN_REPORT_Evolving_the _Customer_Experience_in_Banking.pdf.

18. Tonya Garcia, "Starbucks Has More Customer Money on Cards Than Many Banks Have in Deposit," Market Watch, June 11, 2016, https://www.market watch.com/story/starbucks-has-more-customer-money-on-cards-than-many -banks-have-in-deposits-2016-06-09?mod=mw_share_twitter.

19. "Evolving the Customer Experience in Banking."

20. "H1 2020 Natwest Group Results," Natwest Group, July 31, 2020, https://www .natwestgroup.com/news/2020/07/h1-2020-natwest-group-results-.html.

21. Mike Gamble, "An Experience-First Strategy Customers Can Bank On," Adobe Summit, April 27, 2021, https://business.adobe.com/summit/2021 /sessions/an-experiencefirst-strategy-customers-can-bank-on-s801.html.

22. "The Rise of Mobile Banking in the UK," Global Business Outlook, October 8, 2020, https://www.globalbusinessoutlook.com/the-rise-of-mobile -banking-in-the-uk/.

23. "Digital-First Banking Tracker," Pyments.com and NCR, August 2020, https://securecdn.pymnts.com/wp-content/uploads/2020/08/PYMNTS -2020-08-Tracker-NCR-DIGITAL-FIRST-BANKING.pdf.

24. Sharon Kimathi, "World Fintech Report 2020: 'Traditional Banks Are at a Critical Juncture,'" Fintech Futures, April 21, 2020, https://www.fintech futures.com/2020/04/world-fintech-report-2020-traditional-banks-are-at -a-critical-juncture/.

25. Rozi Jones, "Covid-19 to Increase Demand for Advice over Next Five Years," Financial Reporter, August 13, 2020, https://www.financialreporter.co.uk /finance-news/covid-19-to-increase-demand-for-advice-over-next-five-years .html.

26. "Neobanks 2021: Shifting from Growth to Profitability?" *Inside Financial Services* 5, Exton Consulting, 2020, https://extonconsulting.com/en/wp -content/uploads/sites/2/2020/11/Inside-Financial-Services-Germany -n5.pdf.

27. Rachel Green, "THE GLOBAL NEOBANKS REPORT: How 26 Global Companies Are Winning Banking Customers and Pivoting from Growth to Profitability in a $27 Billion Market," *Business Insider*, January 21, 2021, https://www.businessinsider.com/global-neobanks-report?r=US&IR=T.

28. "World Retail Banking Report 2021," Capgemini infographic, https:// worldretailbankingreport.com/.

29. Dirk Vater, Jens Engelhardt, and Patrick Blaser, "How Digital Done Right Pays Off for Retail Banks," Bain & Company, October 23, 2020, https:// www.bain.com/insights/how-digital-done-right-pays-off-for-retail-banks/.

30. "Five Key Insights from the 2021 Financial Services & Insurance (FSI) Trends Report," Adobe Experience Cloud, n.d., https://business.adobe .com/uk/resources/reports/digital-trends-2021-in-financial-services.html.

31. "Six in Ten Consumers Willing to Share Significant Personal Data with Banks and Insurers in Exchange for Lower Pricing, Accenture Study Finds," Accenture, March 14, 2019, https://newsroom.accenture.com/news/six-in-ten -consumers-willing-to-share-significant-personal-data-with-banks-and -insurers-in-exchange-for-lower-pricing-accenture-study-finds.htm.

32. "Beyond Digital: How Can Banks Meet Customer Demands?" Accenture infographic, 2017, https://www.accenture.com/_acnmedia/Accenture /next-gen-3/DandM-Global-Research-Study/Accenture-Banking-Global -Distribution-Marketing-Consumer-Study.pdfla=en-GB%23zoom=50.

33. Aurelie L'Hostis and Luis Deya, "COVID-19 Stokes the Chatbot Hype in Financial Services," Forrester, September 18, 2020, https://www.forrester .com/blogs/covid-19-stokes-the-chatbot-hype-in-financial-services/.

34. "World Fintech Report 2020," Capgemini infographic, World Retail Banking Report 2021, https://www.capgemini.com/gb-en/news/world-fintech -report-2020/.

35. Open banking: a financial services term as part of financial technology that refers to the use of open APIs that enable third-party developers to build applications and services around the financial institution. (Source: Wikipedia)

36. "Five Key Insights from the 2021 Financial Services & Insurance (FSI) Trends Report."

37. "Capital Markets Day, 2019," Virgin Money UK, n.d., https://www.virgin moneyukplc.com/investor-relations/results-and-reporting/other-events -and-presentations/.

38. Kevin Martin, "Banking Post Covid-19: Five Things That Will and Won't Change," November 24, 2020, International Banker, https://international banker.com/banking/banking-post-covid-19-five-things-that-will-and-wont -change/; "World Retail Banking Report 2021."

39. "Virgin Money Launches Innovative Partnership with Twenty7Tec," Virgin Money UK, December 1, 2020, https://www.virginmoneyukplc.com /newsroom/news-and-releases/2020/virgin-money-launches-innovative -partnership-with-twenty7tec.

40. Duncan Madden, "The Covid-19 Pandemic Has Cost the Global Tourism Industry $935 Billion," Forbes, January 14, 2021, https://www.forbes.com /sites/duncanmadden/2021/01/14/the-covid-19-pandemic-has-cost-the -global-tourism-industry-935-billion/?sh=41563ca27d40.

41. Oxford Economics: The Impact of Covid-19 on the United States Travel Economy, 2020, from Niall McCarthy, "Report: COVID-19's Impact on the U.S. Travel Industry Expected to Be 9 Times Worse Than 9/11," Forbes infographic, April 21, 2020, https://www.forbes.com/sites/niallmccarthy /2020/04/21/report-covid-19s-impact-on-the-us-travel-industry-expected -to-be-9-times-worse-than-911-infographic/?sh=4f57bad25e44.

42. "The Berkeley Hotel in London Delivers Breakfast in Bed at Home," Globe-trender, January 19, 2021, https://globetrender.com/2021/01/19/the -berkeley-hotel-london-delivers-breakfast-in-bed-at-home/.

43. Molly Blackall, "UK Travel Firms Report Sales Boom After 'Green List' Announcement," *The Guardian*, May 8, 2021, https://www.theguardian.com/travel/2021/may/08/uk-travel-firms-report-sales-boom-after-green-list-announcement.

44. Travel to the UK from the "green list" countries is possible without mandatory quarantine at home or at a hotel.

45. Charlotte Marriott City Center homepage, https://www.marriott.com/hotels/travel/cltcc-charlotte-marriott-city-center/.

46. Duncan Madden, "The Covid-19 Pandemic Has Cost The Global Tourism Industry $935 Billion."

47. "Hospitality 'Struggling to Fill Thousands of Jobs,'" BBC News, May 28, 2021, https://www.bbc.com/news/business-57285428.

48. Henn-Na Hotel homepage, https://www.h-n-h.jp/en/.

49. "How Airbnb and Travelers Are Redefining Travel in 2021," Airbnb, October 15, 2020, https://news.airbnb.com/2021-travel-trends/.

50. "Coronavirus Research: Multi-Market Research Wave 5," Global Web Index, July 2020, https://www.gwi.com/hubfs/1.%20Coronavirus%20Research%20PDFs/GWI%20coronavirus%20findings%20July%202020%20-%20Multi-Market%20Research%20(Release%2011).pdf?_ga=2.103308096.1533439618.1626120139-295973798.1626120139.

51. "The Travel Industry Turned Upside Down," McKinsey & Company, September 2020, https://www.mckinsey.com/~/media/mckinsey/industries/travel%20transport%20and%20logistics/our%20insights/the%20travel%20industry%20turned%20upside%20down%20insights%20analysis%20and%20actions%20for%20travel%20executives/the-travel-industry-turned-upside-down-insights-analysis-and-actions-for-travel-executives.pdf.

52. "Hospitality Industry: All Your Questions Answered," EHL Insights, n.d., https://hospitalityinsights.ehl.edu/hospitality-industry.

53. See livezoku.com.

54. Zoku Amsterdam page, https://archello.com/project/zoku-amsterdam.

55. "The Impact of COVID-19 on the Airport Business and the Path to Recovery," Airports Council International, March 25, 2021, https://aci.aero/2021/03/25/the-impact-of-covid-19-on-the-airport-business-and-the-path-to-recovery/.

56. ASQ Barometer, Airports Council International, 2021, https://aci.aero/programs-and-services/asq/voice-of-the-customer/asq-barometers/.

57. Maybe this will be partly or largely based on the hygiene measures going forward. See https://aci.aero/news/2021/03/01/worlds-best-airports-for-customer-experience-revealed/.

58. "How Customer Experience Takes Flight at the Orlando Airport," McKinsey & Company, February 9, 2017, https://www.mckinsey.com/business-functions/operations/our-insights/how-customer-experience-takes-flight-at-the-orlando-airport.

59. "Use of Iris and Facial Biometrics as the Primary Biometric Identifiers for Immigration Clearance at all Checkpoints," ICA, n.d., https://www.ica.gov

.sg/news-and-publications/newsroom/media-release/use-of-iris-and-facial
-biometrics-as-the-primary-biometric-identifiers-for-immigration-clearance
-at-all-checkpoints.

60. "Personal Experiences for 78 Million Travelers," Adobe Experience Cloud, n.d., https://business.adobe.com/customer-success-stories/london -heathrow-airport-case-study.html/.

61. "Delta Will Launch PARALLEL REALITY™ Tech to Serve Up Airport Messages Tailored to Individual Travelers—On a Single Screen, at the Same Time," Delta news hub, January 7, 2020, https://news.delta.com/delta-will -launch-parallel-realitytm-tech-serve-airport-messages-tailored-individual -travelers.

62. "World's Best Airports for Customer Experience Revealed," Airports Council International, March 1, 2021, https://aci.aero/2021/03/01/worlds-best -airports-for-customer-experience-revealed/.

63. "Helsinki Airport Wins Two Awards: Best Airport in Europe in Its Size Category and Recognition for Hygiene Measures During COVID-19," Finavia press release, March 3, 2021, https://www.finavia.fi/en/newsroom/2021 /helsinki-airport-wins-two-awards-best-airport-europe-its-size-category-and.

64. *Improving the Airport Customer Experience* (The National Academies Press, 2016), https://crp.trb.org/acrpwebresource2/wp-content/themes/acrp -child/documents/195/original/acrp_r157.pdf.

65. "Helsinki Airport Development Programme," Finavia, n.d., https://www .finavia.fi/en/helsinki-airport-development-programme.

66. William H. Shrank, Teresa L. Rogstad, Natasha Perekh, "Waste in the US Health Care System: Estimated Costs and Potential for Savings," JAMA Network, October 7, 2019, https://jamanetwork.com/journals/jama/article -abstract/2752664.

67. "The Consumerization of Healthcare," Adobe, February 2019, https:// www.adobe.com/content/dam/acom/en/industries/healthcare/pdfs /adobe-econsultancy-2019-report-the-consumerization-of-healthcare.pdf.

68. "U.S. Hospitals That Provide Superior Patient Experience Generate 50 Percent Higher Financial Performance Than Average Providers, Accenture Finds," Accenture, May 11, 2016, https://newsroom.accenture.com/news /us-hospitals-that-provide-superior-patient-experience-generate-50-percent -higher-financial-performance-than-average-providers-accenture-finds.htm.

69. "The Business Impact of Investing in Experience," Forrester Consulting, June 2018, https://www.adobe.com/content/dam/acom/en/industries /healthcare/resources/pdfs/adobe-impact-of-cx-spotlight-healthcare.pdf.

70. "The Internet of Things: Mapping the Value Beyond the Hype," McKinsey & Company, June 2015, https://www.mckinsey.com/~/media/McKinsey /Industries/Technology%20Media%20and%20Telecommunications /High%20Tech/Our%20Insights/The%20Internet%20of%20Things%20 The%20value%20of%20digitizing%20the%20physical%20world/The -Internet-of-things-Mapping-the-value-beyond-the-hype.pdf.

71. "AI Application for Treatment of Gestational Diabetes," CleverHealth Network, July 3, 2018, https://www.cleverhealth.fi/en/news/ai-application-for-treatment-of-gestational-diabetes-.

72. Stefan Biesdorf and Florian Niedermann, "Healthcare's Digital Future," McKinsey & Company, July 1, 2014, https://www.mckinsey.com/industries/healthcare-systems-and-services/our-insights/healthcares-digital-future.

73. "The Consumerization of Healthcare."

74. Micah Solomon, "Hospitals and Hospitality: What Customer Service and Patient Experience Can Teach Your Business," *Forbes*, April 9, 2017, https://www.forbes.com/sites/micahsolomon/2017/04/09/systems-and-smiles-hospitals-and-hospitality-bu/?sh=697ef29fbb5a.

75. "2020 Year-End Facts and Figures," Cleveland Clinic infographic, https://my.clevelandclinic.org/-/scassets/files/org/about/who-we-are/cleveland-clinic-facts-and-figures-2020.pdf?la=en.

76. "Best Hospitals Honor Roll," *U.S. News and World Report*, https://health.usnews.com/best-hospitals/rankings.

77. *Digital Health Playbook*, Cleveland Clinic Foundation, n.d., https://my.clevelandclinic.org/-/scassets/files/org/landing/preparing-for-coronavirus/covid-response-digital-health-playbook.ashx?la=en&_ga=2.116550470.1149343629.1622380675-69023085.1621684075.

78. Marina Temkin, "Why Some Edtech Investors Could Finally Be Set for a Post-Pandemic Payday," PitchBook, February 12, 2021, https://pitchbook.com/news/articles/edtech-startups-investors-exits-IPOs-venture-capital.

79. See https://info.microsoft.com/Harvard-Business-Review-Education WhitePaper-MGCoo01281.html.

80. Mihaly Csikszentmihalyi, *Creativity: Flow and the Psychology of Discovery and Invention* (New York: HarperCollins Publishers, 1996); Mihaly Csikszentmihalyi, *Flow: The Psychology of Optimal Experience* (New York: Harper & Row 1990).

81. Emily Wasik, "Bridging the Digital Divide to Engage Students in Higher Education," Economist Impact, December 15, 2020, https://impact.economist.com/perspectives/technology-innovation/bridging-digital-divide-engage-students-higher-education.

82. Campus Reimagined page, Florida State University, https://campusreimagined.fsu.edu/.

83. "Florida State University Reimagines Student Learning with Microsoft Teams," Microsoft, March 22, 2021, https://customers.microsoft.com/en-sg/story/1351649898736060046-florida-state-university-higher-education-microsoft365-en-united-stateshttps://customers.microsoft.com/en-sg/story/1351649898736060046-florida-state-university-higher-education-microsoft365-en-united-states.

INDEX

INDEX

CSAT (Customer Satisfaction Score), 65
Csikszentmihalyi, Mihaly, 178
culture. *see* company culture
customer-centric culture, 62–64,
197–98
Customer Effort Score (CES), 65–66
customer experience(s)
development of, 3–6, 19–24, 47–48
expectations vs., 19
measuring, 4, 6, 61–64
customer interface with technology,
34–36
customer lounges, 108
customer loyalty, 22, 113
customer needs, analysis of, 49
customer requirements, 15–16
Customer Satisfaction Score (CSAT), 65
customer service providers, 70–72
CX Index, 45
CYBG (Clydesdale and Yorkshire Bank
Group), 107, 110–11

data
accessibility of, 40–41, 70
in banking sector, 100–102, 105
big, 29
customers' willingness to provide,
35, 101
to develop processes, 196
in education sector, 185
ethical guidelines on collection/use
of, 53
gathering and analyzing, 29, 39–43,
53
in healthcare sector, 152, 154–55,
159–61, 169, 171
in predictive era, 30–34
in travel and hospitality sector, 118
data security, 40–41
delivery, speed of, 200
Delta Air Lines, 141–42
Digital Health Playbook (Cleveland
Clinic), 171
digitalization, 1–25, 191–202
to build relationships with
customers, 17–19
and change in digital-first era, 191–93
and competition, 12–17

and core elements of customer
experience, 19–24
and customer expectations, 24–25
and development of customer
experience, 3–6
ecosystems and platforms for, 7–12
to ensure competence and
customer-centric culture, 197–98
to leverage new technology, 200–202
to manage customer experience,
193–95
as opportunity for businesses and
organizations, x–xi
to optimize processes, 195–97
to set indicators and measure results,
198–200
in stores, 83–84
waves of, 1–3
digital-only banks, 99–100
digital presence, measuring, 63
Digital Trends Report of 2021 (Adobe),
2–3
distribution channels, 9
Dubai International Airport, 140

ease of use, 21–22, 40
eBay, 8, 52
ecommerce, 75
Economist Intelligence Unit, 181
Edge Computing, 32
EdTech companies, 173
education sector, 70, 172–90
case example, 182–90
customer-centric initiatives in, 74
customer data in, 70
learning environments in, 179–81
and learning experiences, 178–79
learning skills for the future, 174–76
role of teachers in, 181–82
student experience in, 71, 176–79
emotional optimization, 18–19
End User License Agreements, 54
engagement, patient, 152, 156–58, 159
Enterprise Resource Planning app,
91–92
Equinox, 124
ethical data collection and analysis,
39–43, 53

INDEX

INDEX

ABOUT THE AUTHORS

SANNA ESKELINEN (MSc in Economics) is a leader with expertise in B2B and B2C marketing. She is recognized for introducing innovative services into markets, building global programs, and leading complex multistakeholder partnerships across the public and private sectors. Sanna is passionate about the impact of technology in different sectors of society and how digital is creating new and changing existing customer experiences. Building on twenty years of experience in the tech industry at companies such as Microsoft and Nokia, Sanna currently works for Adobe and helps to transform the education industry digitally.

She is an avid proponent of diversity, especially bringing more women into the tech industry. She is helping thousands of young people from different backgrounds to find fulfilling work in the tech industry and is an active member of Women@Adobe and a leader of Harvard Women Circles: peer networks that celebrate female voices and the impact they have.

BELINDA GERDT (MSc in Economics) has built a successful international career in some of the world's leading technology firms. She has almost twenty years of experience in developing digital customer-oriented businesses. Currently working for Philips at their headquarters in the Netherlands, she leads global marketing for healthcare solutions and helps digitize the industry. Previously she has worked for Microsoft and Amazon Web Services.

Belinda is a thought-provoking speaker who presents international real-life examples. From her positions at top tech companies, she has observed digital transformation across many industries, enabling and spurring her to follow the latest tech trends and innovations and the role they play in the development of customer experience. This is her fourth book about customer experience management.